Live CAREfully

The Importance of Caring
in a Life of Significance

by
Jerry Traylor

Library of Congress Cataloging-in-Publication Data

Traylor, Jerry.
  Live CAREfully : the importance of caring in a life of significance
/ by
Jerry Traylor.
       p. cm.
  Summary: "Author remembers how caring for others and being
cared for has shaped his life, and tells how caring may shape the
lives of others"--Provided by publisher.
  ISBN 0-9762224-6-9 (alk. paper)
  1. Caring. 2. Conduct of life. 3. Ethics. 4. Traylor, Jerry. I.
Title.

  BJ1475.T73 2005
  177'.7--dc22

                              2005024599

Acacia Publishing, Inc.
1366 E. Thomas Rd., Suite 305
Phoenix, AZ 85014

www.acaciapublishing.com

First printing January 2006. Printed in Canada.

Acknowledgments

I have actually been penning a book for the good part of two decades, but I never had true direction or theme until recently when I answered the question, "Why have I been able to achieve?" The writing of this book has been a great lesson in teamwork and in fact a real microcosm of my entire life. I had a vision, defined my purpose and shared it with others, many who jumped in with open arms to help out.

Thanks to my dear friend, Dwight Johnson, a retired executive who left his position at Chrysler to spend time with his young son Lucas and his wife Laura. Dwight is now a full-time volunteer making a powerful impact through his caring involvement in our community of Fountain Hills, Arizona. Dwight's entire family has held me accountable for this work.

Thanks to Ron Robertson who has a computer consulting business. While working on a computer related problem, he took an active interest in my project and cared enough to provide some upgraded equipment as well as two books which he ordered especially for me about the writing and publishing process. This unsolicited help inspired me to really start focusing on this document.

To my caring sisters, Janet and Debra, who spent extensive hours editing my extremely rough draft. I appreciate the fact that you have always been here for me.

Bill Wotring, yes, the book you envisioned is finally done. Thanks for believing in me so many years!

Tangie Prieskorn, the initial proofreading that you did for me proved extremely valuable. Denny Malone, I appreciate all your technical assistance with the scanning of photographs and the fact that you continued to come around and check on my progress. Finally, thanks to Karen Gray and Acacia Publishing. They have done a great job!

Contents of Caring

Hope Awakens
and Ignites Caring

Thumbs up to Caring People

Running Shorts

Sharing the Mission of Caring

The Caring Life of Jerry Traylor

William E. Wotring, Ph.D.

I first met Jerry Traylor over 30 years ago when a mutual friend arranged for him to speak at the school at which I was principal. He was just getting started in motivational speaking, but he was excellent. The students loved him and he has returned to my schools many times. In addition, I have become a fan of his and have watched him present his message in corporate meetings, in large educational seminars, in numerous churches and at every grade level from kindergarten to graduate school. Jerry always tailors his message to his audience, and participants walk away inspired to reach a higher level of living.

Jerry's entire life is an example of caring. Others have obviously reached out to care for him, and he has extended himself twice as far to reach back to others. Here are a couple of examples.

A few years ago, I had arranged for Jerry to speak at a national educational seminar in Myrtle Beach, SC and was looking forward to his arrival. About noon, I was summoned to take a call from "a Mr. Traylor, who had been involved in a serious auto accident." As I listened, Jerry explained that as he was driving on the West Virginia Turnpike, his car hydroplaned while passing an 18-wheeler and ended up being dragged several hundred feet while underneath the trailer before the driver could get the huge truck stopped. Jerry was extricated through the back seat of the crushed car and rushed to the closest hospital where he was examined and bandaged. Fortunately, his injuries were not too serious, and he was calling to explain what had happened.

After listening to his story and knowing that Jerry Traylor never quits, I (maybe not so caringly) asked if he could get to the regional airport. If he could get a flight, I would pick him up at the Myrtle Beach Jetport. Sure enough, twenty minutes later, he called back to say he had procured a ride to the airport and would be in Myrtle Beach in a few hours.

Jerry cared about his commitment to speak to our group, and, more importantly, he cared about presenting his message to each person who had traveled from all over the United States to be there. After we introduced him as having been run over by an 18-wheeler the day before (thus explaining the bandages on his forehead, arms and hands), Jerry delivered his typical stirring story. Enthusiastic applause is normal following his closing, but this standing ovation continued for nearly 10 minutes. Jerry cared so much that he overcame extensive pain throughout his body to give to others, and they cared so much about him that they gladly would have listened for another hour.

Jerry earns his living as a motivational speaker, but he never passes up an opportunity to make a presentation because the group can't pay him. I have known Jerry to accept numerous engagements knowing his expenses would not even be covered, because he cared about reaching the people. In fact, it has been Jerry's long-time dream to have enough money to do all school and children's presentations without charge.

As Jerry ran across America on his *Trail of New Beginnings*, he stopped in scores of hospitals to see and encourage the children. He remembers what it was like as a child, hospitalized far from home, waiting for days or weeks for someone to visit him. Although his physical body doesn't require him to wait in those hospitals any longer, his memories draw him back to do for others as caring people have done for him.

Jerry Traylor lives a life of caring, and his experiences, both as a receiver and a giver, highly qualify him to present these inspirational stories. Dr. Norman Vincent Peale referred to Jerry as a "motivational doer" in his book titled *The American Character*. Jerry is not only a motivational doer; he is also a "motivational carer."

*Live**CARE**fully* speaks of Jerry Traylor's example of living life fully in a wonderfully caring way.

Foreword: Insights to Caring

Caring has shaped the world, and it has certainly changed my life. Historically, in our early agriculture-based society, caring about one another was necessary for survival. In today's fast-paced, specialized world we generally think of caregivers as healthcare professionals. However, the type of caring I am especially interested in is not so much about our physical needs but about our emotional well-being. The caring I refer to comes from the heart.

Recently, when I arrived home from a speaking tour, I discovered that a dinner of roast beef and mashed potatoes had been placed in my refrigerator. The givers were obviously Candy and Jerry Caldwell as they are the only ones who have access to my house. The meal was greatly appreciated, as I had just returned from Alaska and in only two days would be leaving for Colorado. During such quick stopovers at home, I generally head to the local drive-through windows as it seems impractical to go grocery shopping for such a brief period. The Caldwells' gesture touched my heart, and when I reached into the freezer to find my stash of coffee, I saw that Candy had even topped off my meal with some Häagen-Dazs ice cream. This went far beyond any expectations and left me standing alone in my small kitchen in tears.

The act of caring can be tremendously powerful. Though it may not take a great deal of time or effort, unexpected thoughtfulness can have a profound significance. The feelings of love, of caring, of belonging that I felt when finding that delicious meal shall never be forgotten.

Throughout my life, others have cared for me in thousands of ways. The high expectations of my mother Marilyn and father Tom were vital to me. The gentle nudging of my three loving sisters, Janet, Judy and Debra has proved valuable in ways that I could not understand at the time. Many dedicated professional healthcare providers and educators touched me as they rendered their services. Hundreds of other close friends and casual acquaintances have given unselfishly to help me on my roadway of life.

We often see the greatest caring when we are at our weakest. It was natural for many people to reach out to care for me, a handicapped child. But it also seems that at those times when I have had incredible visions — when I've had a dream and have taken the initiative, such as running across America — others have wanted to be part of that vision.

Throughout my life, God has given me a stage on which caring could be played out. Early on, others saw a frail, weak child with cerebral palsy. If I fell, it was natural for them to run and pick me up. I was praised for the two or three faltering steps that I took before falling. Later, those around me would forget about my imperfections and quickly tell others that they had seen a guy running, dancing or playing ball on crutches. This opened doors to many opportunities. Interestingly, this caring was quite unconditional as those around me cheered the participation rather than evaluating the results. I have never won a marathon, but I have been highly praised for participating and demonstrating the determination to finish.

I am thankful for the realization that I didn't have to fit in with the group. Ironically, the very thing that kept me from fitting in was the same thing that allowed me to stand out. No matter what I did, my crutches assured that I would be noticed. I was different. I didn't even have to try to be unique. This visibility gave me the arena that allowed me to have an impact on others. Yes, I was noticed, and I hope that one thing that most people noticed was that I also cared about others.

As a motivational speaker, my intent has never been merely to give a speech. Rather, my intent is to help people change their lives. The purpose of the platform God has provided to me is not to get listeners to look at me. Rather, the real value comes when I can prompt people to look at themselves. I pray that this book will have the same significance.

Over the past 20 years of my speaking career, I have often been encouraged to write a book. Following one corporate sales meeting, the manager even said that if I had had a book, he would have purchased a copy for everyone in the audience. That kind of book sales would have doubled my income for the session, but something did not feel right about doing that. I felt that my real strength was in personal appearances, in the opportunities to see people face-to-face. I wanted people to come to know me not as a hero on paper, but as a real person.

The letters and feedback that I have received have supported this belief; audiences have thanked me for being there. Not just for being there physically, but for being there emotionally as we cheered, faced challenges, and cared for one another. Over and over, I have experienced the value of personal exchanges, often while sitting down to lunch with friends or new acquaintances and expressing mutual caring.

I have always wanted folks in my audiences to see their potential. The important message was never Jerry Traylor's accomplishments. The real message came in explaining *why* Jerry was able to achieve. It was in helping others see how caring individuals helped transform me from a handicapped child into a caring, capable adult.

While most of us will never be inducted into the Hall of Fame for Caring Americans — yes, there is one, located in Washington, D.C. — we must realize that genuine caring does transform lives. This book honors individuals who have touched my life. My hope is that as you journey with me through these pages, you will reflect on what caring has meant to you. I want you to experience a heartfelt gratitude for those special people who have been there for you, in both your difficulties and your joy.

Throughout this book, more than 200 caring concepts serve to distill each chapter's message. Each concept offers an example of the many avenues of caring that surround us.

I also challenge you to look at your life and its significance. Have you truly utilized the gifts that God has blessed you with to serve and empower others? At the end of each section of this book is a questionnaire designed to assist you in this introspection. And, finally, I will ask you to share your personal stories of caring — who has touched you, and who have you touched?

It is my desire that we all learn to *Live**CARE**fully*.

Jerry Traylor
Fountain Hills, Arizona

Hope Awakens

and Ignites Caring

Until We Meet Again

The hospital ward was our home. At any given time there would be 10 to 14 of us recovering from medical procedures. The nurses in this children's ward were so very caring, treating a lot of pain that went beyond the physical. Many kids were traumatized when they were left in this unfamiliar place.

Dinner time at the hospital. Jerry, age six, is in the striped shirt.

We built friendships like an internal neighborhood. Among the difficulties could be heard laughter as we played

3

games or assembled puzzles. We had visitors, though we were seldom good hosts. The hospitality came from those that entered the dark building. Many came just to care. Cousins and more distant relatives on my mother's side were often there, prompting a smile as they handed me a card or a gift.

Every now and then a person like Roy Rogers or Dale Evans would walk through the door. The stir they created was powerful. The difference they made went well beyond the silver screen. Now, it is fascinating to look at the lyrics of "Happy Trails," the theme song from the Roy Rogers show. The words so clearly tell the hopeful tale of a child confined in the hospital.

Some trails are happy ones,
Others are blue.
It's the way you ride the trail that counts,
Here's a happy one for you.

Happy trails to you,
Until we meet again.
Happy trails to you,
Keep smilin' until then.

Who cares about the clouds when we're together?
Just sing a song, and bring the sunny weather.
Happy trails to you,
'Til we meet again.

As I looked around the ward, I knew that I was blessed. I remember one little guy that I would stare at as he hungrily spooned food into his mouth. He was only four years old and did not yet know how to read. I was six, almost seven, and I eagerly waited for him to finish his meal so that I could read my newest book to him. I was fortunate. I knew it as my hands picked up the book.

As he ate, my little friend held his spoon between his toes. He had no hands. He had no arms. He had only one leg. It may be that my friendship and reading helped him, but his very presence in that lonely ward showed me early on that I could care and give, and that I was truly blessed.

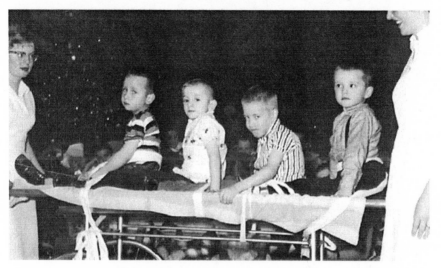

Jerry at four, sitting on a stretcher, third boy from left.

Caring can be learned while young.
Caring is something we all need at times.
Caring allows us to focus on our blessings.
Caring allows us to experience joy in difficulty.
Caring transcends celebrity status or boundaries.

Points to Ponder

What is your earliest recollection of someone caring about you?

What is your earliest recollection of making a difference in the life of another person?

Has anyone cared for you who had nothing to gain?

Talk about your earliest realization that you were blessed.

Sowing the Seeds of Caring

The apple has long been a symbol of health and wellness in our society. It has also been used by Madison Avenue to symbolize our country, as in the slogan "As American as apple pie." America's largest city is even known as the "Big Apple."

As a child I often heard the familiar saying, "An apple a day keeps the doctor away." I would consume bushels of this fruit hoping that was true. But, no matter how many dumplings, fritters, turnovers and pies I ate, I would repeatedly end up in the doctor's office, facing yet another corrective procedure on my cerebral-palsied legs.

I remember as a first grader, polishing an apple to a brilliant shine. I presented it to my teacher because she let me know that I was also capable of shining. Mrs. Traphagen created a classroom climate that made me eager to learn. She always looked for and expected her students' best, which caused me to polish that apple with pride so it would be pleasing to her. She instilled good feelings and happiness in her students. I have long realized that when others believe in us, we begin to believe in ourselves.

Jerry with his first grade teacher, Mrs. Traphagen, in front of East Ward Elementary School in McCook, Nebraska.

I have also discovered that a bushel of assorted apples tends to reflect society. In many ways, our national diversity, as well as our personal self-images, is represented by the many varieties of apples. For example, in the classroom, the apple tends to reflect the uniqueness of each student. We all strive for the brilliance and level of excellence of the Red Delicious apple. However, some teachers and parents do not help students realize their potential. Some children, with limitations or individual difficulties, may feel like a blemished apple hanging way out on the far end of the family tree. As a child, I sometimes felt like others were bright and shiny, but that I could not mix with the brightest apples. I guess that many of us feel inadequate at times; more like applesauce than a Delicious apple.

In reality, most of us fall into the class of apples that would be graded as average — perhaps, like the Jonathan or the Paula Red apples. We try to fit in, hoping to be accepted and useful. We may feel slightly blemished or even a bit wormy at times. We do our jobs, but we are not expected to be the sweetest or juiciest.

Examining the relationship between apples and humanity, we can notice further parallels. There are apples that reflect our diversity of ethnicity such as the Fuji, the Rome Beauty and the Macintosh. There are those that are more mature like the Granny Smith. Some of us are very gifted like the Pineapple or stand out like the Cameo. There are even those of us who tip the scale on the moody side like the Crab Apple. And some of us are hardly known, like the Summer Rambo.

Overall, there are over 2500 varieties of apples in the United States. The smallest is about the size of a cherry and the largest is bigger than a grapefruit. Our uniqueness, like that of apples, should be nurtured and praised, yet it seems that we often are judged against the Criterion.

My teacher realized that I was worthy of her best efforts — that I was a valuable apple that could be polished and nurtured to become more like a Delicious apple. Her job was tough! Too often, our teachers feel overwhelmed when they try to teach a child who may seem spoiled. The child may smirk, disrupt the classroom and assert negative pressure on others. In fact, sometimes a teacher may feel that she has been stuck with too many rotten apples. Today, I certainly appreciate Mrs. Traphagan's belief in me, and the extensive efforts she put into trying to make a Delicious out of a physically imperfect specimen.

A teacher must think of a problem student as a doctor evaluates a patient in severe pain. She must look for the source of the problem. There may be a lack of parental guidance and positive role models in the student's life. There may be domestic problems or critical economic conditions. To influence others, we need to understand each individual's situation. We must get to the core and then replant good seeds.

In the late 1800s, Jonathan Chapman fell in love with apples. Traveling throughout a large area of the United States, "Johnny Appleseed," as he became known, sowed the seeds of his favorite fruit everywhere he went. The Jonathan apple is named after this crusader. In like manner, we must plant positive seeds everywhere we go — the seeds of hope, compassion, integrity, friendship, spirituality and love.

Tending apple orchards and caring for one another have several similarities. Planting seeds is only the first step. We must then cultivate one another with words of acceptance, tolerance and encouragement.

Occasionally, apple trees need to be pruned to ensure that the tree's nutrients and sunlight can reach the fruit. We all need to prune our own unhealthful habits so that our desirable qualities can flourish.

And, like all living things, orchards and humans need proper nourishment and fertilization to assure that they grow to their full potential. This is as true of children as it is of those more advanced in years.

Did you know that an apple tree cannot produce fruit from the pollen of trees from the same variety? There needs to be cross-pollination from a tree of a different variety. We are somewhat like that. Working with people of different backgrounds and cultures can help us grow more richly than staying among just our own type.

Apples and people — so many varieties to enrich our lives.

Caring nurtures rather than ignores.
Caring means waiting for the harvest.
Caring means increasing our tolerance.
Caring celebrates uniqueness and diversity.
Caring can change an environment, a future.
Caring is looking beyond the grief, to the glory.
Caring is something that needs to be cultivated.
Caring includes others that may not measure up.
Caring acts as a fertilizer, enhancing our growth.
Caring is patient, getting to the core of a situation.

Points to Ponder

Name a person early in your life who really believed in you and helped you believe in yourself.

If possible describe a particular incident that was life-changing.

Can you name a time when you first learned about diversity?

The Transformation of Caring

I remember waking up as a six-year-old from an ether-induced sleep in the darkened recovery room after yet another in a series of corrective operations. I was in great pain, a state with which I had become all too familiar. My mother sat next to the bed, gripping my hand. Glancing up at her, I caught a tear rolling down her cheek. Any emotion which she may have felt was overshadowed by her optimism as she said, "Jerry, one of these days, things are going to be better."

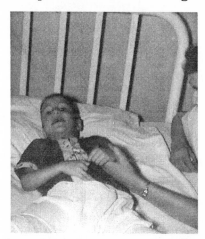

Living 240 miles away from the hospital, Jerry's mother (holding his hand, at right) could visit only every two weeks.

My parents taught me not to feel sorry for myself, but to accept each new challenge with the idea of trying my best. If nothing else, I could at least come away from a challenge saying, "I tasted the agony of defeat." At best, I would reach a new level of achievement.

My elementary school reports indicated that at times I was not focused on the classroom work, or perhaps, that I marched to the beat of a different drummer, but I, at least, got in the parade. I often appeared to be a square peg trying to fit into a round hole. My ABC's may have been more about Acceptance, Belonging and Caring than what the

13

teacher had in her lesson plans. I so desperately tried to fit in.

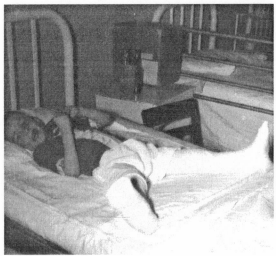

Six year old Jerry spent 11 1/2 months in the hospital having several of what would ultimately be 14 surgeries.

I am thankful that my parents helped me establish a need and desire for independence. Some parents pick their children up and carry them rather than letting go of the leash a bit to allow their child to learn difficult lessons through life's experiences. I was expected to do my part around the house and to finish the household chores that every child bemoans.

I learned that I could contribute; in fact, I was expected to contribute and to do my part. That lesson served me well as I became involved in high school activities. As a sophomore at South High School in Pueblo, Colorado, I enjoyed going to all the sporting events, and the school generally fielded good teams. One week, Rocky Sisneros and Bert Stjernholm, co-captains of the football team, honored me with the school spirit award. I was asked to lead the pep rally and to sit on the team bench during the games. That gesture molded my school years and quite possibly changed my life, since I subsequently participated with many teams as the student manager.

Being part of a team was meaningful. I felt that I was making a difference and contributing where I could. During practices, I helped with details and at games I performed many managing tasks. Going on road trips was exciting and the cheerleaders honored me by putting spirit banners on my locker just as they did for the players. My entire social life seemed to revolve around athletics, yet I had never scored a touchdown or sank a shot from the baseline. My senior year was exciting, as we won 19 basketball games during the regular season. We entered the state tournament ranked third but were beaten in the first round by the second-placed Panthers of Harrison High in Colorado Springs.

❧❦

Caring is optimistic.
Caring is spirit-filled.
Caring catches our tears.
Caring strives to achieve.
Caring stresses teamwork.
Caring will grip your hand.
Caring teaches difficult lessons.
Caring fills a dark room with hope.
Caring often marches to a different drummer.

Points to Ponder

Describe a time that you cared so much that it brought tears.

Has there ever been a time where you felt you did not belong, and a caring individual reached out to embrace your participation?

A Careful Walk

On April 20, 1974, I learned that I could push beyond anything I had experienced, that I could find value in helping others, that I could be an active participant in all that life has to offer, and this feeling has never left me. After reading a newspaper story, I decided to participate in the March of Dimes Walkathon. The March of Dimes catered to the needs of children with birth defects. I felt thankful for my mobility; in gratitude, I wanted to help others.

Following is the experience, in my Mother's words:

"I now laugh at the time Jerry, shortly out of high school, showed his interest in self-punishment. He signed up for a 21-mile walkathon to benefit the March of Dimes. Jerry had never attempted anything remotely this challenging, and I feared for his well-being. It was a hot, windy day and I was afraid that he would collapse in the heat.

At one point, he was crossing a viaduct with a strong wind whipping around. Unbeknownst to him, I was following and tried to stay out of his sight. My worry heightened as he struggled against the wind. He looked totally bushed. I finally pulled along side of him, rolled down the window and pleaded for him to get in and ride home. He was adamant and not about to bring his quest to an end. I should never have interfered because he was at the 19-mile marker by this point and only two miles from the finish. But, Mother always knows best — right?

I remember how the crowd reacted that day. They were amazed at the strong-willed young man on crutches. I guess that I was right there with them. I was in awe. How could my son be doing this? I had seen his struggles, his pain, and his tears. Now, I was seeing his victory. Proudly, I took his picture; I had to have proof of this event or his grandparents would never believe it. By the way, 2,597 walkers participated and Jerry raised more in pledges than anyone else. This experience proved to be an indication of his future successes and an example of the continual caring that was ingrained so deeply in his soul."

Sue Stearns, Executive Director of the March of Dimes, was quoted in the newspaper as saying, "Jerry was blistered from fingers to elbows from the extended exertion. We asked him to stop at the third checkpoint but he refused. He wouldn't even stop to rest, he just kept going."

Caring means participating.
Caring continues the quest.
Caring leaves others in awe.
Caring battles the headwind.
Caring is ingrained in the soul.
Caring goes beyond the known.
Caring is captured in our memories.
Caring is indicative of future success.
Caring brings opportunities to others.

Points to Ponder

Sometimes real caring means letting go so that a person can grow in their own independence. This is difficult. Have you ever dealt with this dilemma? Talk about it.

Name a time when you embraced a cause to the extent that your involvement took you to levels that you had never reached. Was it worth it?

A Heavenly Dance

In May 1974, after successfully completing the March of Dimes Walkathon, I was asked to participate in a six-hour dance marathon for the March of Dimes. That sounded like a fun challenge. Two years earlier, as a high school sophomore, I had learned that dancing could be part of my repertoire. I had invited Janie Shaffer to the homecoming dance. In hindsight, it must have been a bit awkward because I had never danced. Actually, I had never been on a date.

My sister Judy and her future husband Byron chauffeured us to the dance. Janie and I followed the example of most as we sat passively against the wall. I believe it was the Led Zeppelin tune *Stairway to Heaven* that prompted Janie to ask me to dance. Though I had never danced and was a bit self-conscious, there was no way I could refuse such an invitation. Today, I am still grateful that Janie drew me onto the dance floor, and realize her compassion as I reflect on the experience. Though I was the only one on crutches, she didn't seem to care. She did not question whether I could dance. Janie looked like heaven. It was not long before I learned that I could cast aside one crutch and place my free arm around Janie. Believe me, I never looked back!

Caring means trying new things.
Caring is a bit of Heaven on earth.
Caring allows us to dance with joy.

Points to Ponder

Name a time when you tried something that you had never done before.

Did a particular person prompt that action?

What effect did making the effort to move outside your comfort zone have on you?

Burned Out

It was just past midnight on February 25, 1975 on a bitterly cold morning when I was awakened by desperate pounding on the door of my room in Robidoux Hall at Western State College in Gunnison, Colorado, where I was a freshman. Rushing down the hall, the alarmists frantically yelled, "The building is on fire! The building is on fire! Get out!" Most of us did not even grab personal possessions; thinking it was just another college prank. When we gathered in the lobby of the neighboring complex, we quickly realized that this was no joke. We felt helpless as we watched through the frost-covered windows at the horror before our eyes.

The temperature was 15 degrees below zero, and this numbing weather made the task of fighting a fire very difficult. There was also a great emotional burden added as the firefighters realized that not only were a lot of possessions being destroyed, but the loss of life was also a real possibility.

A policeman at the side of the building was shooting out windows. Thick, black smoke billowed out. One fire hose called the "Black Widow" pushed 1,200 gallons of water a minute into the fire, but it was no match for the raging flames.

Mrs. Marjorie Childs, resident director, quietly took a roll call, and the rumor began to spread that someone was missing. A student had heard coughing, which seemed to be coming from the third floor. The word spread that it was a firefighter coughing. Then, Dan Street, one of the resident assistants, saw a student near a third floor window and yelled for him to jump. Fellow student Mark Horch actually went back into the building to save the person, but was driven back by the intense heat and smoke.

Though we knew a resident was still in the building, we also understood that rescue was impossible. In those conditions, a human could not survive for long. Risking

ROBIDOUX BURNS

An on-campus fire claimed the life of one WSC student and destroyed the third floor of Robidoux Hall on February 25, 1975.

Brett Reid, a freshman resident of the third floor of the dormitory which provided housing for 132 men, died of smoke inhalation. The remaining 131 residents were able to vacate the building safely.

The fire was first discovered about 12:30 a.m. by residents of the building, in an alcove equipped with facilities for ironing clothes. Attempts were made to put out the fire with water and a fire extinguisher, but Resident Advisor Sam Desantis soon recognized the need to vacate the building.

There was no panic as students worked to assure safe exit of their friends. Student resident advisors received high praise for supervising the orderly evacuation.

Temporary housing was immediately provided for the residents of the hall. "The response of students and townspeople to this unfortunate situation has been most gratifying," President John Mellon said. "We received many calls from people, organizations, and businesses of the community offering to open their homes and provide other help, and the supply of clothing and even textbooks was quite impressive." Local and Denver representatives of the Red Cross were also on the campus to help.

Robidoux Hall is part of a three-dormitory complex which provides housing for 417 men, mostly freshmen. The newest buildings on campus, the complex was first occupied in 1966.

26

another's life would be foolhardy. Eventually, the roof caved in. Two hours later, the body of freshman Brett Reid was recovered.

Most of us hung around the lobby all night, weary from the horror and too wound up to sleep. Daylight brought an eerie silence. The sub-freezing weather had sculpted a sheet of ice, which cascaded from the burned-out building.

I was touched by the way community members opened their loving arms to offer homes and to provide material items. The Red Cross helped provide replacement clothing, emergency medical supplies and over $7,000 worth of new books. I was amazed that over half of the clothing offered to us came from caring citizens.

It was a challenging freshman year. The fall quarter had introduced the loss of life to me. In rather rapid succession, my grandfather Don Walter and a close family friend had died. My cousin, a young man who had much going for him, took his own life. And Brett Reid had perished in our dorm fire. I was deeply affected by this because I had just played a round of golf with Brett the day before the fire.

My freshman experiences shaped my thinking. I had participated in a March of Dimes Walkathon and a dance marathon in Pueblo. I had been involved in helping others in need, and had also been on the receiving end of a community's caring following the dorm fire. The deaths, the value of life, the value of community were speaking to me. I felt that I was being called to act, so I organized a dance marathon to help repay the Red Cross. I suddenly became known for being proactive rather than bemoaning our losses. I was still a freshman, but these events shaped my philosophy that God can use each of us in great ways if we focus on our potential rather than our immediate situations. Human beings tend to look at probabilities, while God opens up possibilities.

Caring creates community.
Caring can be a profession.
Caring may permit survival.
Caring grows in the cared for.
Caring brings many factions together.
Caring is heightened during uncertainty.
Caring allows even average people to give.
Caring makes its presence known in tragedy.

Points to Ponder

Have you or any of your acquaintances ever been involved in a tragedy in which an entire community came together in caring?

How did it shape your thinking or your life?

The Butte-i-ful Journey

By 9:00 on a beautiful Sunday morning, Donna Adams and I had crossed the Gunnison River and were starting up another hill on our day-long hike from Gunnison to Crested Butte, Colorado. We were hiking along the highway to raise money for the Gunnison Valley Council for Exceptional Children.

We were both singing to the tunes that flowed from my backpack radio. The morning church hour with Pastor McKnight had ended and some of the most fantastic songs ever heard were now being played.

By the Time I Get to Phoenix did not seem quite fitting, although this hike was becoming a long, hot trip. *Oh, What a Beautiful Morning* seemed better. Later, *Raindrops Keep Falling on My Head* was appropriate.

Donna and I had covered a little over four miles when the first bicyclists caught up with us. The next couple of miles dragged on slowly. We kept singing and talking as we trekked along the warm asphalt, enjoying the birds' songs and watching the cattle in the green pastures to the sides of the road.

As we trudged on, another cyclist, Sandy Anderson, caught up with us and stopped to talk for a minute. Donna and I were becoming weary and our conversation waned as we concentrated on moving forward. Rain set in and we shivered in the unspeakable chill. A mallard duck rose in solitude from the roadside stream.

We were beginning to think that maybe we were truly crazy for undertaking such a goal when another student drove up to remind us of why we were there.

"Think of the beauty of it all," Debbie exclaimed. "Remember the purpose and the many special-needs children we will help. We're helping to make summer programs, field trips and arts and crafts possible with the money we're raising."

Donna and I cared so much about the Council for Exceptional Children; she was Vice-President and I was President, and we knew the value of the programs. We were thrilled at the opportunity to help our children, although at that moment, we would surely have enjoyed a long rest.

As our walk continued, the rain ceased and the sun came out. The road seemed terribly long and it generally seemed that no one knew what we were doing as they sped by in their cars without so much as a wave or acknowledgment.

By noon we had reached Almont and were resting over iced tea. I phoned KGUC radio in Gunnison to let them know that a group of caring individuals was doing a good deed for the day. The bicyclists were riding five to six hours; Donna and I were facing a much longer day.

After nearly 11 miles, we were feeling the burden of the uphill, high-altitude trail. Gunnison lies at 7700 feet above sea level and now we were at 8412 feet. Our destination was Crested Butte, at 9000 feet. The disc jockey began reminding people traveling toward Crested Butte to be on the lookout for participants in the bike/hike. He exhorted, "These people are doing a great job, so show your appreciation by stopping to talk to them or by honking and waving." That prompting helped as drivers began to honk. In fact, a couple of geese also honked as they flew over. Donna was inspired as she spotted the snowy butte, our goal, looming nearly 20 miles up the highway.

By 2:00 p.m. our movement was slowing. Donna and I sat down a couple of times and were barely able to get back to our feet. The bikers had completed their ascent and returned to Gunnison. We were left alone without comrades to cheer us on. More than once, I almost lost my head and nearly decided to lie down and roll back down the mountain, but Donna's spirits urged me to continue the climb.

A couple of hours later, Crested Butte lay only 10 miles ahead, while Gunnison was 20 miles behind. Just as I came to the conclusion that nothing could stop me, Donna was thinking of giving up. Her throat was sore and her stomach was upset. But even as we were wilting, a miracle happened. J.W. Campbell, a Western State college administrator, appeared and invited us for some coffee and cake at his nearby in-laws' house. Donna and I collapsed on the chairs around the food-laden table and enjoyed the cake. In fact, I felt no guilt at all as I took a second piece, rationalizing that I needed the nourishment for the seven remaining miles. After cake, coffee and a Coke, I was ready for anything.

It was 6:15 p.m. and we had been on the road for 10 hours. We were definitely weary, but we had to make it. Some friends came to check on us and to encourage our last few miles. After completing a couple of miles, I decided to bring this journey to an end as soon as possible. I began jogging as fast as I could, leaving Diane with her friend Dan. I knew that at that pace I could finish in an hour. The time passed quickly until a woman stopped to take my picture silhouetted against the setting sun. She was a reporter from the *Crested Butte Chronicle* and explained, "You have become our celebrity by climbing all the way from Gunnison to Crested Butte on crutches."

Although I wasn't carrying my backpack any longer, I was still carrying my crutches. Actually, they were carrying me as they had since shortly after those childhood surgeries had corrected my twisted legs and allowed me to move with freedom as a "normal" person does.

The last mile of the climb was something I shall never forget. A woman came out of her house and offered refreshing water. I burst into tears as I climbed that final, long hill. An hour earlier, I did not know if I was capable of making it, but finally, it was downhill the rest of the way. I knew that within five minutes I would be sitting in my friend Randy LaPorte's red Mustang waiting for Donna and Dan to come over the hill. As I ran past the city limit sign, I tossed my crutches to the ground and stumbled to Randy in tearful and agonizing, yet joyful, victory.

The photographers were ready to take more pictures as Donna and Dan reached the goal. Donna and I embraced with tears of joy. Donna's feet and my hands were covered with blisters, but the pain was secondary to the satisfaction we were experiencing.

A half hour later, we were back in Gunnison, amazed to think that the highway we had just labored over could be covered in such a short time by car. I arrived home, putting an end to the longest, yet possibly the most beautiful day of my life. For years, I had tried to find ways to inspire and to help others. In high school, I had answered phones at the Jerry Lewis Muscular Dystrophy Telethon. Most of those children were confined to a wheelchair. I had been blessed with mobility that enabled me to hike for 12 hours up a mountain highway. I was not only thankful for two good legs, I was thankful for a precious life that I could share with others.

Caring is contagious.
Caring eases burdens.
Caring loves company.
Caring heightens hope.
Caring can inspire action.
Caring is not always easy.
Caring creates opportunities.
Caring becomes easier if it is noticed.
Caring helps us focus on what we have.

Points to Ponder

What kind of civic, social, student or church organizations have you taken an active part in? Describe a particular time when your participation made a positive impact. By any chance did you gain more than you gave?

That Takes the Cake

During a journalism class while attending Western State College, one of my assignments was to interview someone and to write a feature story. As you have probably realized, I tend to look at the extreme possibilities rather than finding an easy way to finish a task.

I decided that rather than interviewing a local professor, mayor or the oldest resident in town, I would find someone more widely celebrated in the media. I had heard that Lyle Alzado, an all-pro defensive lineman for the Denver Broncos, would be appearing in Denver at a benefit for the Special Olympics. Realizing that such a busy individual would probably never receive my message and give me an appointment, I decided to head for the Mile-High City benefit, search out Mr. Alzado and ask for a moment of his time.

Saturday morning, I found a ride to the Marriott Hotel in east Denver. It was easy to spot my target. I was immediately impressed with the interaction Lyle had with his eager fans. When I first saw him, this Herculean athlete was in the middle of a desperate arm-wrestling duel with a giggling child. You can imagine who won the contest. I asked Lyle if he would be willing to grant me a twenty-minute interview. He graciously agreed but stipulated that I would have to talk to him between the charitable matches.

What a pleasure it was to talk to this man who had gained a reputation as one of the most vicious pass rushers in the National Football League. His educational background intrigued me. Lyle had majored in special education at tiny Yankton College in South Dakota, which explained his gentleness toward the children who gathered around him. My feature story focused on the seeming irony of the gentle giant who was feared by so many on the field.

After lunch, I noticed that Mr. Alzado had moved to another part of the room and had taken on the role of chief barker at the cake auction. The home-baked cakes were going for amounts ranging from five dollars to well over $40.00. The bidding on a delicious-looking chocolate cake had just opened as I walked toward him. When Lyle asked for an opening bid, I playfully offered a pitiful figure of $1.68. Without hesitation, my new friend announced, "Sold to Jerry Traylor for $1.68!"

I somehow managed to find a way to carefully pack the gooey treat in my backpack as I hitchhiked back to Gunnison. Drivers who stopped to offer me a ride got a piece of delicious cake — more than they had bargained for.

Footnote: I met Lyle Alzado at a benefit for Special Olympics, whose motto is, "Let me win, but if I cannot win, let me be brave in the attempt." Lyle Alzado loved winning and did a great deal of it in his storied football career. His last battle though, an off-field battle, is where he showed his true bravery. But he could not win against brain cancer, losing the ultimate battle in 1992 at just 42 years of age.

Caring can be sweet.
Caring has no appearance.
Caring often draws a crowd.
Caring comes in unexpected ways.
Caring may give the victory to others.
Caring can bring out the gentleness in anyone.
Caring means validating those who are weaker.

Points to Ponder

Talk about a well-known person who has exhibited a great deal of caring.

Did his or her caring deeds become a major media event or were they downplayed?

THUMBS UP TO CARING PEOPLE

Hitchhiking disclaimer: *In this day of heavy drug use and increasing violence, I would never condone standing along a road thumbing a ride. An individual is totally defenseless against a potentially lethal piece of metal moving down the road at a high rate of speed. Even if there were no evil intent on the part of the driver, there is always a real possibility of an accident. Just a light brush from a moving vehicle at high speed would be enough to kill an individual. Once in another person's car, if the driver is dysfunctional, escaping alive from a moving vehicle or defending against a deadly weapon would be unlikely. Therefore, I no longer practice, advocate or condone hitchhiking.*

I will state that as a young man in my twenties, I greatly enjoyed the adventure of hitchhiking and the different strategies employed to get rides all over the United States. I met some wonderful, caring people on the road that I would never have come into contact with any other way.

Thanksgiving after Christmas

Was I crazy or what? I had left my home in Parkersburg, West Virginia nearly 14 hours earlier. I was now in the heart of Virginia, entering the historic city of Richmond. There was little chance that I would actually see history being made, and I really didn't even feel that this day would go down in the annals of my memory as I walked along the cold streets leading to Highway 60 and Virginia Beach.

The sun sparkling off the whitecaps as they danced against the golden sand was my vision of a beach, any beach. This reality was a long way off — even further than the 110 miles that separated me from my destination. The truth of the situation was all too evident in the bitterly cold air piercing my body. It was about 5:00 in the morning and only those with the schedule of a milkman can fully appreciate the deep quiet of the deserted streets at such an hour, especially on the day after Christmas.

The holidays were behind me. I had spent Christmas at the home of friends Ralph and Marcia Lowery. I was blessed to have many friends that welcomed me, a single guy, into their festivities. I really cherished the joy of being with families, the laughter of children, and the delicious aroma of holiday potpourri simmering on the stove. Why would I choose to leave such warmth for the cold streets?

At times, my constant journeys became a game. Four months earlier I had decided to run an organized foot race every weekend for an entire year. Not owning a car many years ago, my transportation was by thumb. I was at the mercy of others, and quite frankly, as I walked along those frozen, desolate streets, it seemed as if there was no mercy.

My last ride had picked me up a couple hours earlier on Interstate 81. He had left me at the interchange heading east. I was now dealing with one of the greatest challenges faced by a hitchhiker. Since most of the traffic as you approach a city is local, and of little help in making measurable progress, it would often take hours to get through the congestion and back to the open road. Given the early hour and the 23-degree weather, I knew that it would be a tough go.

Footsteps approaching from behind brought me out of deep reflection. A voice piercing the predawn darkness called out, "Hey, man, where ya headin'?"

"I'm trying to hitch a ride to Virginia Beach," came my weary reply.

"That may be hard at this hour. Why don'tcha come up to my place and warm up?" said this fellow in a southern accent.

I had always been trusting, more than most, as evidenced by the fact that I was out on the road in the first place. But NO WAY! I couldn't just walk into the house of a stranger in a disheveled, unfamiliar neighborhood.

"Oh, c'mon, I just live in the projects right up the hill," he prompted.

I would have to be crazy, I thought to myself. I mean, I know nothing about this fellow. Why is he outside at 5:00 in the morning? Probably coming home from a party somewhere, I figured.

With caring and pride this guy said, "Hey, man, I'll make you a turkey sandwich. My mama has a lot of leftovers from Christmas."

Proving that anyone has a price, I followed this fellow, who introduced himself as Tim, up a sloping sidewalk to a complex of matching brick buildings. As I mounted the steep stairway and climbed to the second floor, I still harbored a great deal of uneasiness. If trouble lay ahead I was not fast enough to dash down the steps to safety.

The first thing I noticed as we entered the dwelling was an open door at the end of a hall. A man, probably in his sixties, lay in a bed. Tim said, "That's my daddy. He's paralyzed. I gotta work two jobs to support my dad, my mom, my wife and two kids."

Within minutes, a feast, unlike any breakfast I had ever had, adorned the Formica kitchen table. Silence dominated as I sampled a turkey sandwich on white bread along with some stuffing and mashed potatoes that had been warmed in the oven. My gaze inched its way around the room, the cracks in the ceiling, the torn linoleum on the floor, the stark loneliness of a simple refrigerator and gas stove with no modern appliances to keep them company.

Tim's voice startled me, "Now, ya see how us folks live." I was embarrassed in knowing that I had been caught gawking at the humble existence of this family.

With pride, Tim continued, "Yep, man, ain't we lucky? We get to eat Mama's cooking all the time."

Suddenly, it really didn't matter whether I caught a ride on down the road to run in that ten-mile race. I felt privileged to be part of the human race. Even though the weather was bitterly cold, I realized that the human spirit is so wonderfully warm.

Caring takes chances.
Caring removes doubts.
Caring provides comfort.
Caring embraces strangers.
Caring celebrates humanity.
Caring is wonderfully warm.
Caring transcends conditions.
Caring means working two jobs.
Caring means bringing together.
Caring knows no skin color, only the human race.

Points to Ponder

Has an unknown person ever attempted to help you and you had to decide whether to trust this person? Talk about this incident.

It certainly may be a safer choice not to trust, but if you chose to trust, explain your feelings, the outcome, and any lessons you may have learned.

Talk about a time when your fear or prejudice has kept you from learning.

The Window of Fear

Our media don't often enough feature stories of the incredible caring nature that is inherent in human beings. Throughout my life, I have found that most people genuinely want to ease the burden of those who are in need. In the arena of hitchhiking, these people, at least twenty years ago, were prevalent. Given the uncertainty involved, it may have been a risk to pull to the side of the road while offering a non-perfect stranger access to your vehicle, but quite a number of people did so.

It was about 3:00 on an August afternoon, and I was walking along Interstate 70 near Columbus, Ohio. As I reached the side of the small car that had pulled onto the shoulder of the road, I heard a frail voice asking if I was okay. I stated that I was on the way to the airport to catch a 7:45 p.m. flight bound for Colorado. Fear was obvious as this timid black woman indicated that she was worried about me out there all alone in the stifling humidity. She said that she wanted to help me but that she was terrified and didn't know if she should give me a ride.

Though it was difficult to communicate through the passenger window that was cracked a full inch, I told this lady that whatever decision she made was acceptable. Her continuing fear was evident as she said, "I really do want to help you, but I am afraid." I assured this caring individual that I would be fine even if she chose to pass me by.

In a wave of uncertainty, she continued to express her concern. "I know how dangerous it is to pick up a hitchhiker. I have never done this before, but you are on crutches, and I don't think I should leave you out here."

"Ma'am, I appreciate your concern. You have to do whatever your heart tells you. I will be all right," I assured her.

After several more moments of discussion, this anxious lady nervously unlocked the door and asked me to get in. We introduced ourselves, and I learned that Mary was on her way home from work. I really empathized with her uncertainty as she punctuated her conversation with continual glances toward the backpack that lay across my lap. Finally, Mary said, "Can you please put that pack in the backseat? I'm afraid you might have a gun or something in there."

As I got out at the airport, I thanked Mary for caring enough about my well-being and safety to deal with the enormous fear that she felt. I also asked that she continue to exercise caution in similar situations.

With an incredible sense of gratification, I decided to celebrate the spirit of this caring moment by splurging at the fancy restaurant on the upper level of the airport. While enjoying a superb entrée of stuffed flounder, I couldn't miss the spirited conversation two tables over.

It was apparent that a girl about eight years old was having a birthday dinner with her mother. Still basking in the afterglow of Mary's loving gesture to me, I wanted to give something to someone else. I asked the waiter to deliver a big piece of chocolate cake and a Shirley Temple drink to the birthday girl, along with a note saying, "The love, joy and laughter I have witnessed coming from your table this evening has been a blessing to me. I hope that your birthday has been equally joyous to you."

Our country was built on a spirit of giving and service to others. This caring spirit is still very much alive.

Caring may be scary.
Caring should be celebrated.
Caring gives birth to good feelings.
Caring is something we all want to do.
Caring may enter through a narrow window.

Points to Ponder

Has there been a time when you saw a person who might have a need but you did not know how to respond or were scared to help? Explain.

What did you finally do?

How did it make you feel?

My Run on Broadway

Like most days in the life of Jerry Traylor, I really had no idea what was unfolding. It was another adventure following yet another unknown path.

When 3:00 came on that Friday afternoon, I had eagerly grabbed the pack that lay beside my desk and headed out the door. I was working as a claims examiner for the U.S. Treasury Department in Parkersburg, West Virginia and the extended Columbus Day weekend gave me a chance to explore more of the unfamiliar East Coast. A traveler named Ron had relieved me of hitchhiking with a ride near Carlisle on the Pennsylvania turnpike. It was now nearing 6:00 on Saturday evening.

We were traveling through a seemingly endless tunnel, which had robbed us of the lively tunes that were playing on the radio. The light in the tunnel was dim and all was quiet except for the purr of the vehicle's motor as we neared our destination.

My palms were sweaty and my breathing quickened as we emerged from the tunnel. I was overwhelmed! Many a dreamer had pictured it: the Big Apple, the glittering lights of Broadway, the Great White Way. "Yes," thousands have declared, "If I can make it here, I can make it anywhere." The reality of the moment was, however, far from glamorous. The first images beyond the calm of the tunnel were nearly heart stopping. A sea of humanity was rushing by, its rhythm accompanied by the ever-present blare of a dozen taxi drivers tuning their horns. Looking up, all I saw was an imposing wall of concrete that blocked out the evening sky.

As Ron dropped me off on the corner of 42nd Street and Broadway, the sights, the sounds, and even the very smells that rose from the streets of this city were almost too much to handle. Suddenly, I found myself in the midst of the city that never sleeps, on an island the size of ten large farms in my native rural Nebraska. I was sharing this limited space with over eight million people. (Nebraska's entire population is only one and a half million.) I was definitely experiencing maximum sensory overload.

I was apprehensive as I walked up the narrow staircase of the seedy-looking hotel, which lay within shouting distance of Times Square. Several bottles were strewn haphazardly in the hallway. Upon glancing around the room, it quickly became apparent that this humble hotel room and its mattress, the consistency of a marshmallow, were not where I wanted to spend my evening.

Escaping the hustle and bustle of Broadway, I ducked into a quiet establishment featuring a piano bar. Quite often when traveling solo, I tend to eavesdrop on the conversations around me. A couple was talking about lighting and sound, and as my curiosity and fascination were piqued, I boldly asked if they worked on Broadway. My suspicions were confirmed when the fellow said that he was the stage technician and that his companion played the lead role of Cassie in the long-running Broadway hit *A Chorus Line*.

The woman, Deborah Henry, obviously had incredible passion for her craft as she spoke of her role on Broadway and the path she had traveled to success. At the end of our conversation, Deborah offered to get me tickets to the next evening's production. I felt a great deal of disappointment as I turned down her gracious offer because I had to leave the next afternoon to have a good chance of getting back to my workplace by Tuesday morning. Deborah encouraged me to call her on my next visit to the city.

Six months later, my mother flew from Colorado to meet me in New York City for a vacation. Prior to leaving my home in West Virginia, I called Deborah Henry to tell her that we would be in the city and would love to get together. Deborah proved to be a woman of her word, remembering her offer to treat me to my first Broadway play. She stated that two tickets would be waiting under my name at the will-call window of the Shubert Theatre. She also asked us to meet her after the performance in her dressing room back stage.

The production was intense as the cast of characters portrayed the reality of what they had experienced in the casting call. There was the fear of a misstep, possible rejection, and the rare victory that was within the grasp of only a few. Much like the character she portrayed, Deborah Henry had come to New York with a dream to make the big time. Her path began many years earlier in a small Tennessee town. Starting out in her junior high school play, Deborah eventually left home to tour with the Royal Winnipeg Ballet in Canada. The dance lessons she had started as a ten-year-old were finally beginning to pay off.

After the performance, Deborah welcomed us with open arms to her private dressing room. As we sampled wine and cheese, Deborah asked if there were any other Broadway productions that we would like to see. I was in awe as she suggested *Pirates of Penzance*, with Linda Ronstadt and Rex Smith, as well as *Sugar Babies,* starring Mickey Rooney and Ann Miller. Deborah stated that complimentary tickets would again be available for me. In parting, she autographed a *Chorus Line* booklet with the words, "Thanks for your inspiration and happiness. Love, Deborah Henry."

Both productions were exhilarating. Mother was especially thrilled as Mickey Rooney brushed by her as she sat along the aisle prior to *Sugar Babies.*

The entire experience left me grateful for this warm and loving woman who had befriended me, providing something that only another human being could offer in the midst of this crowded concrete jungle. Her gesture has remained etched in my mind since that day, nearly two decades ago.

I later had the opportunity to work in Manhattan for a few months. During that time, I called the Shubert Theatre in an attempt to locate Deborah. The person I talked to had no idea where she was. Over the eight months that I held the position in New York City, my heart told me to continue my quest to find her. I felt it was important to let her know how much her actions had meant to me so many years ago.

As so often happens, we put things aside and don't follow through as we might. I never did re-connect with Deborah. Soon, I packed my belongings and moved to Arizona to build my speaking career.

Some months later, I was back in the northeast again, this time to give a speech for Public Service Electric and Gas Company in New Jersey. One afternoon, I took the train into New York City.

As we clattered forward on those tracks I had ridden so often before, the past suddenly confronted me. I was grateful that a departing passenger had left behind a copy of the *New York Times*. It had been nearly two years since I had had the opportunity to read "all the news that's fit to print." I was struck instantly by the headline, "Deborah Henry, 44, Broadway Dancer." The article told of her struggle and ultimate loss to the effects of ovarian cancer.

Deborah Henry, 44, Broadway Dancer

Deborah Henry, a Broadway dancer
who appeared in *A Chorus Line* and
a number of touring musicals, died

on February 5 at her family's home in Memphis. She was 44 and lived in Union City, New Jersey.

The cause was ovarian cancer, said Donna Drake, a friend.

Ms. Henry danced with the Royal Winnipeg Ballet before becoming a musical theater performer. She traveled throughout the country with the New York and touring companies of numerous musicals, including *Promises, Promises* and *Cats*, but she is best known for her work in *A Chorus Line*, in which she performed so often that she was sent out to prepare new touring companies for the show.

Chorus Line legends clung to Ms. Henry, including one about her persistence in completing the high-powered dance number *Music and the Mirror* while bats flew around her head in one Midwestern theater. She is survived by her father, Jack; her stepmother, Christine; two brothers, Michael and Jack; a sister, Darlene, and a stepsister Ashley, all of Memphis.

Many recall the passion of Deborah's dance performances. My mother and I were fortunate enough to be partners in her dance of life for a couple of evenings. Thank you, Deborah Henry! The importance lies not in the power and passion of your staged performance, but rather in the passion you gave to others through the way you lived.

Deborah went well beyond the call of duty to reach out in an expression of human love, leaving me with a favorable first impression of New York City. She was in a position that few achieve, having starred in *A Chorus Line* since opening night in 1975. Yet she never became egotistical or standoffish. I was a complete stranger, a hitchhiker — she had nothing to gain through her generosity to me.

Deborah, I only wish that I had given a little more effort to locate and thank you. It is with irony that I read your obituary and found that your Broadway debut was in *Promises, Promises*. It didn't matter to you if I arrived in the Big Apple by way of my thumb. You delivered on your promises to a small-town boy and his mother and deeply touched our lives.

Caring actions are so prevalent in our great country, and I am thankful for the opportunity I have had to meet so many giving individuals. Deborah Henry showed such genuine caring. I am sure that I said thank you to Deborah after her kind gestures to me, but I am not convinced that my gratitude was sufficient. It is important to let others know that their efforts are meaningful and possibly even life-changing. Did she ever realize how much her giving touched me?

Caring means sharing.
Caring means being generous.
Caring means expressing gratitude.
Caring means keeping your promise.
Caring is about making someone's day.
Caring means giving without conditions.
Caring means going beyond expectations.
Caring for others assures you will be missed.

Points to Ponder

Describe a time when a total stranger gave you a gift or facilitated a kind gesture.

How did it make you feel?

Did you offer appropriate gratitude?

Friends on the Roadway of Life

One thing that my miles of hitchhiking have brought me is a great many friends, a few of whom have stayed in touch to this day.

Pat and Janet Greer

In preparation for a 30-hour dance marathon at the University of Northern Colorado, in which I was scheduled to participate, I had hitchhiked up to Greeley to hustle pledges for the event. My partner Brook and I, both Western State College students, had set a goal of raising over $3,000 and felt that people would be more willing to give in the host school's community.

I had registered for the event, and was wearing the green April Fool's Dance Marathon T-shirt as I headed back to college in Gunnison. Pat Greer, a salesman for Walker Electronics Company in Greeley, picked me up just south of Greeley. Pat was traveling only to Brighton, but in our short ride together he pledged one dollar per hour for the upcoming 30-hour Muscular Dystrophy Association benefit. Pat also said that he would show up at the University during the event to say hello and to offer his support. Many people make promises in this busy society, so I really had no expectation of seeing Pat at the dance. It was two weeks later, at about 11:30 Saturday evening, after nearly twelve hours of tiresome dancing, when I was given a pleasant lift as Pat and his wife Janet walked into the crowded ballroom.

At 1:00 in the morning, we were given an extended break of six hours. (Colorado state law mandates that any dance marathon over twelve hours must have a certain amount of

Jerry and a partner at one of his many dance marathons.

time allotted for rest.) Pat and Janet were still in attendance and asked if my dance partner and I would like to spend the short night at their home. It was such a blessing to sleep in beds rather than in sleeping bags in the middle of a hard gymnasium floor. We were even given a home-cooked breakfast which energized our weary bodies for the second half of our endurance endeavor.

That evening, after the dance came to an end, the Greers once again opened their home to us. This world is filled with special people who really desire to make a positive difference. It is hard to relate to a soul trusting enough to pick up a hitchhiker, and it really stretches us to think that someone would go to the point of giving a cash contribution, two nights lodging and two great meals to support the efforts of someone they hardly knew.

By the way, Brook and I placed first in the marathon, dancing the entire 30 hours and procuring over $4,200 in pledges, which would be equivalent to about $12,000 today.

Caring means getting involved.
Caring means providing a place of rest.
Caring means getting on the dance floor.
Caring means helping the less fortunate.
Caring means telling others of your mission.
Caring provides for the well-being of others.
Caring means supporting the efforts of others.

Mr. and Mrs. Randolph

I was hitchhiking from Gunnison to my parents' home in Pueblo on a Friday afternoon, when a middle-aged couple picked me up and shuttled me over Monarch Pass before dropping me off near their home in Salida. As we passed the Monarch ski area, they asked me if I had ever skied on my crutches. I answered in the affirmative, and they proceeded to tell me about their son who, after losing a leg to cancer, had become a competitive skier using outriggers, crutches with short skis at the base. Unfortunately, he had recently passed away.

The method their son employed was called three tracking, because of the three tracks left on the snow, a short ski at the base of each crutch and a regular ski on the remaining leg. My form, of course, is called four tracking as I use the crutch-based skis and a ski on both legs. As they slowed the car to let me out, Mrs. Randolph asked if I would have any use for their son's outriggers and a couple of pairs of crutches. Their giving spirit continued, as they offered me a bed in their home, should I ever get stranded at dusk in Salida.

Caring gives others a chance to contribute.
Caring means being available when needed.
Caring remembers the past and focuses on the present.

Art and Sybil Richards

It was way too late in my eyes and as black outside as the coal that was so common in the surrounding hills. I was only 60 miles from my home in West Virginia, but it may as well have been a thousand miles. My last ride had left me at the side of the road at 8:30 that night, more than two hours earlier.

Down the road, perhaps, a half-mile or so, I spotted the taillights of a car glowing brightly and giving away the intentions of the driver. It seemingly took forever, but finally the small car was near me. I only wished that an additional witness had been present, as I really feel that this individual may have qualified for the Guinness Book of World Records as the "longest distance covered while backing up for a hitchhiker."

The driver stated that it was virtually impossible to see me walking along the road in the darkness. Sensing my movement, it was an afterthought that someone along the road might need a ride or other assistance.

During the short trip into Parkersburg, we introduced ourselves and talked a bit, but in reality, I was so exhausted that I retained very little of what was said. My ride was kind enough to deliver me right to my front door.

Approximately two weeks later, I got home from work to find a note on my door from "Art Richards" who said that he was passing through Parkersburg and wanted to see how things were going for me. For the life of me, I could not figure out who Art Richards was or when I may have met him. Art was kind enough to leave an address and phone number, and asked that I call him if I was ever near his home in the Columbus, Ohio area. Shortly thereafter, I was in Columbus to participate in the Scioto Downs Run for Life to benefit the American Heart Association.

The evening before the run, I dialed Art's phone number and he agreed to come out to the Scioto Downs racetrack the next morning to say hello. I don't know why, but I didn't have the nerve to tell Art that I could not recall meeting him. Possibly, when we met in person, I would recognize him or he would drop some hint that would help unravel the mystery of our meeting.

Art was already in the parking lot when I arrived after getting a ride from a friend. This balding man strolled over to me and offered a healthy handshake and a welcome smile. Embarrassingly, I still had no recollection of meeting this man. After introducing me to his wife Sybil and other initial talk, I felt that I could no longer conceal my lack of memory. I hesitantly said, "I'm embarrassed to admit this, but I don't recall where I met you."

Art recapped the night when he picked me up at the Interstate 70 and 77 interchange. He told me of how he had backed up to offer a ride after barely catching a glimpse of me that dark night. I immediately remembered the ride, and realized that due to my weariness, Art's name did not settle into my mind. At any rate, recognition would have been difficult after initially meeting under such dark circumstances.

Art laughed as he described his fascination upon meeting me. I had said that I was hitchhiking home following my participation in a race that I ran on crutches. Art said that his initial thought was that I was able-bodied and that I participated in some fad or craze of running races with crutches. He did not realize my true physical limitations until our second meeting in the Scioto Downs parking lot.

The Richards became very dear friends in the next few months. I got to the Columbus area frequently and maintained close contact, often staying in their home. Art and Sybil have become part of a very special network of surrogate parents to me as they have shared their wisdom and support in so many ways. They are both extremely caring individuals who are deeply involved in the ministry of their church. Following the untimely passing of their son John to cancer, Art once said that I was the only son that he had.

I greatly admired the diversity that Art cultivated in his life. During his retirement following a career as a salesman for a pharmaceutical company, Art kept busy as a long-distance truck driver, working for a collection agency, and giving private piano lessons to a number of individuals. Art was also blessed with an incredible gift of music composition, and was kind enough to compose a touching song that he played during my wedding ceremony. Thank you, Art, for caring enough to take a chance on a weary hitchhiker on a dark night. You and Sybil have brightened my world.

Caring is HEART-felt.
Caring creates family.
Caring goes out of the way.
Caring is a like a joyous melody.
Caring lights the way for others.
Caring offers appropriate follow-up.
Caring sees the need in the darkness.
Caring backs up when it has gone too far.
Caring is remembered even when names aren't.

Points to Ponder

Have you ever reached out in caring to someone who you did not know? (other than through charity work involvement)

Was your involvement deeper than just a simple act?

Have you ever lost a loved one, but because of his or her life, you were able to help another?

Do you routinely keep an eye out for those who might need your assistance?

Have any of these strangers that you helped, or those who aided you, become lifelong friends?

A Run of Peace

The race: International Peace Race, Youngstown, Ohio
25 kilometers (15.6 miles), November 10, 1979

This event was called the International Peace Race; however, peace was being tested about that time with the hostage situation in Iran. It was truly an international race as runners from 18 countries participated. I roomed with a runner from Nigeria. There was much talk between the athletes about representing their countries in the 1980 Olympics.

For this race, I was just hoping to break three and one-half hours. The day was hot and the course through Mill Creek Park was hilly. When I crossed the finish line in 3 hours and 13 minutes, I was totally exhausted and must have looked like I was dying. Due to numbness, I could not feel my hands on my crutches, and I nearly collapsed at the finish line. Some volunteers led me to an ambulance and the medical technicians directed me to lie down. They re-hydrated my body and in a short time I was feeling better.

After chatting with these medical professionals for awhile, I mentioned that I needed to find a way back to my motel, which was slightly over ten miles away. The medical technicians said that they would take me, and told me to just lie back and relax. I lay back on the stretcher and away we went. Upon arriving at the motel, I started to sit up, but they would not let me. They opened the rear doors and wheeled me on the stretcher right into my room where they slid me off the stretcher and onto the bed.

I later called the front desk to ask what time it was. Ignoring my question, and with obvious anxiety, the motel clerk asked if everything was okay. When I said I was fine, she asked about the ambulance that had just been there. I replied, "Ma'am, there is no need to worry. I always travel that way!" She was not convinced until I walked to the office to prove that I was all right.

Caring eases worry.
Caring restores health.
Caring is international.
Caring promotes peace.
Caring takes you where you need to go.

Points to Ponder

Describe a time when an emergency, medical or otherwise, brought caring professionals to your assistance.

Tell about a time when others went beyond the call of duty to care for or about you.

Thanks to the Caring

The race: Thanksgiving Day Race, Cincinnati, Ohio
10 kilometers (6.2 miles), November 23, 1979

As Thanksgiving approached, I saw an ad in *Running Times* magazine for the Cincinnati Thanksgiving Day run. I called the number listed and spoke to Don Connolly, race director. I was disappointed when Don told me that registration was closed. I explained that I was in the midst of a goal to run a race every week for an entire year and that I ran on crutches due to having cerebral palsy. Don made me chuckle with his reply: "You what!? Run on crutches?"

Don was fascinated by my story and eagerly invited me to come over to Cincinnati and participate in his race. Since I was traveling so much, I told Don that I could really use help with lodging if he knew of any runner who would be willing to put me up. The next day Don called back and said that a fellow by the name of Pete Looney and his wife Diane were willing to provide lodging. This was especially nice since this was the first year I was living so far from my family in Colorado.

The race ended in Riverfront Stadium, home of the Cincinnati Reds and Bengals. My 65-minute time was a personal record by over four minutes. I was called to the microphone in that enormous stadium where I had the opportunity to express my personal gratitude. My remarks triggered a standing ovation. The moment was certainly meaningful to me.

The trip to Cincinnati became an annual tradition, and each year a different family chose to host me, so I had many opportunities to make new friends. All of us tend to take for granted that we can sit down at a Thanksgiving feast each year. In this case, I broke bread with friends, most of whom I had not previously met, who were willing to take me into their homes. Their graciousness demonstrated the true spirit of Thanksgiving.

Caring stands and applauds.
Caring celebrates Thanksgiving.
Caring provides food — for thought.
Caring should be shared with others.

Points to Ponder

Have you ever reached out to involve a single person in your family holiday activities? Do you make this effort outside of the holiday season?

Talk about a time when others may have included you in their activities.

The Birthday Flight

Orthopedic Equipment Company which was head-quartered in nearby Bourbon, Indiana, had been supplying my crutches at no charge for some time and surprised me with a birthday cake, a monogrammed jacket and a new pair of crutches at the finish line. Happy belated birthday!

I was featured in the newspaper, which mentioned that I had hitchhiked to this race. During my birthday celebration, a fellow approached me and said, "Jerry, I read in the newspaper that you hitchhiked up here from West Virginia. My wife and I live down there and are heading back. Would you like a ride?" I, of course, readily accepted the invitation. A few minutes later, we were heading down the road when Mr. Slaughter flicked his signal and turned right. As we slowed to a stop, he said, "That is our plane over there." Yes! My ride back was in their four-seat private plane which was much more expedient than putting out my thumb.

࿐

Caring means celebrating life.
Caring is something you can lean on.
Caring is a present wrapped with love.
Caring means lifting others up and giving them wings.

Points to Ponder

Name a time in your life when an act of caring was so unbelievable that it left you speechless.

What is the birthday present that you have received that represented the most caring? (This may have been because it was homemade, or took some real time. Likely we are not talking about a material gift.)

Running with Dad

The race: The New York City Marathon
New York City, New York, 26.2 miles, October 25, 1981

The New York City Marathon ranked right up there with the Boston Marathon as far as the prestige involved. Race Director Fred Lebow had made some very adamant public comments forbidding my participation in this event; however, the truth was that he did not even know that I was among the mass of 16,000 runners standing on the Verranzano Bridge waiting for the starting cannon.

Six months earlier, I had met Tracy Sundlun at the Cleveland Revco Marathon. Tracy was a member of the Warren Street Social and Athletic Club which is based in Jersey City, New Jersey. As you might imagine, this club is about partying as much as it is about running and athletics. Tracy went back home and told the WSSAC membership about me. They promptly sent me a WSSAC T-shirt and wrote, "As an honorary member of the Warren Street Social and Athletic Club, you will wear our T-shirt during the New York City Marathon." They further stated that they were prepared to take legal action if I were not allowed to run.

As it turned out, they had me fill out an official application for the marathon and submitted it with their stack of applications. My entry was processed and approved without race committee knowledge of the Lebow concern or the fact that I was on crutches.

My father, Tom Traylor, had flown in from Colorado to watch me in this marathon, which turned out to be a very special treat for both of us. The day before the race, while

81

wandering through the hotel race headquarters, I introduced Dad to several runners including Alberto Salazar and Allison Roe who both had a reputation for winning. I felt privileged to have met many gifted athletes on the running circuit which to my amazement had welcomed me so warmly. I told Dad to be on the lookout for Salazar because he might very well win the marathon in world record time.

As it turned out, Salazar and Roe both set new world marathon records. Some 16,000 runners started the race, which weaved through five boroughs of New York City. Starting atop the Verranzano Narrows Bridge in Staten Island, we headed into Brooklyn, where we passed many small children who reached for our hands and seemed to idolize us. Further on in the same borough, the inquisitive and stern gaze of the Hasidic Jews wearing their black hats greeted us. We proceeded across the Queensboro Bridge leading into the multicultural neighborhoods of Queens, into Manhattan, Harlem, on into the Bronx, and finally back into Manhattan and the upper-class high-rises that served as home to the wealthy and famous. It was fascinating to experience such a diversity of cultures along the way. The path to the finish in Central Park proved to be quite hilly and a real challenge.

My time of 5 hours and 37 minutes was good enough to beat 300 of the 13,000 runners who finished, none of which used crutches. It was my best time of the year but really took a lot out of me. Ruth Rothfarb, an amazing 80-year-old woman, finished just seconds in front of me. I had seen her on the course the last few miles and had doggedly pursued her, but each time I got near she would put on a little sprint and shake me.

The finish line of the 1981 New York City Marathon where two world records were set. Jerry (and his Dad) crossed the finish line much later.

Dad was so excited as the public address system announced my approach that he breached race rules, ducking under the yellow security tape and charging onto the course; he actually crossed the finish line right behind me. It was a highly emotional moment for both of us.

In his youth, my father had received all-conference status as a football player at the rural small school level. He was excited when the doctor pronounced my arrival; "It's a boy!" Visions of athleticism must have momentarily flashed through his mind before the realization that I was handicapped finally struck him. He witnessed incredible struggles and had likely felt incredible, undisclosed pain during my childhood years. Now, we embraced at the finish line of the New York City Marathon! I had completed the same race that had produced two world records.

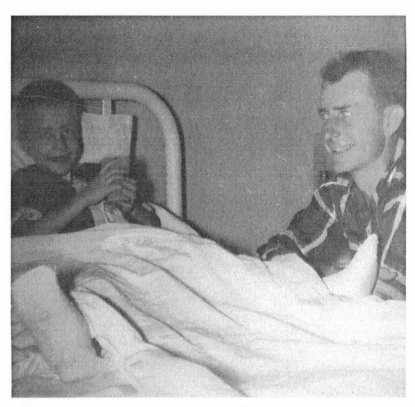

During early hospitalizations, Jerry's father Tom could only dream of his son's eventual achievements.

Dad had arrived at Central Park early and had secured a spot in the Finish Area spectator bleachers for the duration of the marathon. He told me that boredom was never a problem as he watched, encountered and spoke to both the rude and the friendly in this incredible city. He enjoyed telling about the lady seated next to him who even offered him some peanuts and homemade spinach pie.

After leaving the Big Apple, we traveled to Atlantic City where we stayed in a motel about two blocks from the ocean. Dad was miffed that the washcloths were made of a paper fiber. He went to the office and let them know that, "Even in the small town in Nebraska where I come from, we have washcloths which are made of cloth." He got what he was hoping for as the manager soon appeared with "real" washcloths. We went to several casinos with no luck. Dad seemed particularly fascinated by the street signs, as Atlantic City had been the model for the Monopoly board. Our motel was actually on Pacific Avenue, and Dad had me take numerous pictures of him posing under street signs for the wooden Monopoly board he hoped to create.

After a couple of days in Atlantic City, my father and I rode a bus to Washington, D.C., where I was scheduled to run the Marine Corp Marathon on Sunday. On Wednesday evening, after checking into our hotel in Arlington, Virginia, we took a taxi across the Key Bridge into Georgetown. While walking down "M" Street, we were intercepted by a young man who had dashed out of Tony's Steakhouse. He said, "Mr. Leming wants to know if you are the guy who ran the Marine Corps Marathon last year on your crutches." After answering, we followed the employee into the restaurant where Ernie Leming, his wife and another couple were just finishing their meal.

Ernie said that he was inspired by my effort in the marathon the previous year. I found out that he actually served on the race committee. He asked if I had had a chance to see all the sights in our nation's capitol. I told him that I had been there many times and had seen most of the sights, but that this was my father's first visit to the area. Ernie stated that he would like to provide a tour for us. "Be down in the lobby of your motel at 9:00 tomorrow morning."

The next morning as we stepped off the elevator, a fellow wearing a uniform, walked toward us to ask if I was Jerry Traylor. He said the limo was waiting outside. WOW! Mr. Leming had promised a tour, but there was no way we were expecting that a chauffeur-driven limousine would be at our disposal for the next five hours. We were driven just about everywhere. When we circled the nation's capitol and White

85

House, tourists gawked to see who could possibly be riding in back of that fancy automobile. Our chauffeur drove us to a restaurant near the National Zoo, and said that he would be waiting when we finished. My father would have none of that. "Where I come from, we all eat together," Dad said. He insisted that Jim join us, and he paid for his lunch. The chauffeur thanked us, saying, "In all my years of work as a chauffeur, no one has ever been so gracious as to include me as you have." We had an incredible tour that neither of us would ever forget.

Friday evening, October 30, I spoke at the pre-race seminar. Dad left the next morning, and I still cherish the memories of those experiences together. Dad cared about me. I felt pride in demonstrating my athletic achievement for him — and especially for being his son.

Caring creates no monopoly.
Caring means meeting others.
Caring means preserving hope.
Caring means showing courage.
Caring stands for what is right.
Caring allows everyone to participate.
Caring means letting someone else win.
Caring means going to bat for someone.
Caring means giving a world class effort.
Caring means getting on the starting line.
Caring means providing a warm washcloth.
Caring means showing pride in your children.

Points to Ponder

Talk about a quality time that you shared with your father, perhaps a time where the caring was pervasive and provided a time of real bonding.

Discuss a time when someone went to bat for you to make sure that you were included.

Describe a time when you felt pride as you watched your child participate in a program, athletic event or other endeavor. Also, share a time when you were thankful that your Dad or Mom was present to see you accomplish something.

SHARING THE MISSION OF CARING

When we encounter speakers, they typically have come from the athletic field or the business world. They are well known for their successes and many, more common people, want to "rub elbows" with such achievers. These individuals just naturally start sharing their stories.

I was speaking well before I achieved anything of note. I was an activist trying to promote positive action and change. It was because of this need for action that I began to speak. I actually walked the talk before talking the walk!

As you have read, for me, the mission of caring began at a young age. The very fact that I needed help drew others to me as they watched over my well-being. This impacted me greatly and you have read the stories of how I have had the opportunity to give back.

Perhaps the event that really lead me into a leadership role was the dormitory fire my freshman year at Western State College. While others bemoaned their material losses, I began a campaign to express my thanks to those who came to our aid. My efforts drew the attention of many and before long I was encouraged to run for student council and other leadership positions.

In October 1976, I was invited to participate in the Colorado Governor's Conference on Handicapped Individuals. While at this conference in Denver, I was nominated to represent the state at the President's White House Conference in Washington, D.C. The attendees would elect ten delegates and part of that process was a speech from each nominee.

There I was, a college student, in front of over 300 individuals in that crowded ballroom...my first experience at public oratory. It was from that platform that I learned that I had a gift. My words flowed easily, but I truly believe that I was elected to go to Washington, D.C. for another reason. Those in the audience could see that I cared!

It was not the gift of gab that carried me to Washington as part of the Colorado delegation, it was the simple caring that was so evident. The audience felt my compassion, not only from the words that touched their hearts, but also by the time I spent learning about *them* during the remainder of the conference.

My confidence was lifted and my resume was enhanced during that process, and speaking invitations began to come my way. Soon those in the corporate world were calling me to address their functions. I brought a real-life story and hope to those who faced incredible challenges.

Visionary Caring

Vision, strength, goal-setting: I had addressed them all in my 35-minute message to the Marietta, Ohio Rotary Club. I had shown images from my life on the screen. For some reason, God had given me the gift of moving people from vague thought into action. My own life was the example of how I had faced challenges as a youngster and had persevered to become an athlete.

Three months prior to my presentation to his Rotary group, Tom Fenton had witnessed the real-life inspiration during the ten-kilometer Parkersburg Road Run. Despite the ten-minute head start given to me by the run's organizers, Tom and other more physically gifted runners had eventually passed me on the course. It must have seemed odd to come upon a guy pushing his body along the road with mighty arms dragging feeble legs.

Tom had been inspired and asked me if I would address his Rotary Club. It was during this message that I suggested that one day I would like to jog across America, raising funds to benefit the elderly and the handicapped. Following my talk, Tom said that he would like to support my journey. "Let's get our Marietta Rotary Club involved. Let's get Rotary International involved. In fact, let's set up a meeting and talk about this." I think that I swallowed my tongue at that moment. I wish that I could have seen the look of panic on my face. "You mean I really have to do this?"

A week later, I received the following letter from Tom Fenton:

Dear Jerry,

Thanks again for coming to Marietta to tell your story to our Rotary Club. I wish you could have listened in on the many comments I have received since. "Congratulations. Excellent program. Inspirational. Best program we have ever had. First time a non-official ever received a standing ovation here."

And, read what our Club bulletin editor wrote about your appearance:

> *"Pittsburgh, New York, Denver, Fiesta Bowl and Pikes Peak — an impressive list of marathons for any runner to boast. When the runner's movement is aided by crutches, those credentials tax the limit of one's imagination. But 'limit' does not apply to Jerry Traylor. He will never know the meaning of the word."*
>
> *Jerry used a graphic slide autobiography to portray 14 years of hospitals, operations, pain and courage that finally overcame cerebral palsy, and allowed movement in braces and then crutches.*
>
> *Jerry says, "You learn to make the best of what you have." So, "looking for something to do one day," he entered a three-mile race — and finished. Four months later, he completed his first marathon and began a great story of courage and adventure.*
>
> *More than a runner, Jerry Traylor is an attitude -- adventure, curiosity, challenge, dedication, and sacrifice -- bolstered by a wry sense of humor that permits hope for each new day. "Most of all, don't feel sorry. I realize there are others in worse circumstances who can use my help," says Jerry.*
>
> *In 1985, Jerry will run from Los Angeles to New York to raise funds for the handicapped and the elderly.*

Tom's letter continues...

Jerry, I spoke with our Rotary President, Charlie Foshee, about your 1985 coast-to-coast run for the handicapped and elderly, and I asked him whether Rotary International could help you. He was interested and asked if you and I could define for him exactly how money would be raised and disbursed, and how the elderly and handicapped would be involved along the way. If we could do this, then he would be glad to bring the idea before the Rotary Board of Directors for review. Maybe your run won't ultimately involve Rotary, or even service clubs, but evaluating feasibility could be a useful step to build on. Let me know what you think.

Kindest regards,

Thomas K. Fenton, Vice President
Fenton Art Glass Company

I was used to receiving kudos for my speaking. It always felt good to have my speaking gift validated. I never get tired of making a difference. It was the additional content in Tom's letter that chilled my bones. The line saying, *"Limit does not apply to Jerry Traylor... He will never know the word's meaning."* Hearing this caused me to realize that perhaps I had spoken out of turn.

I had expressed a vision, a sincere desire to jog across our great country. Now that vision was in front of the world. It was in the Rotary newsletter, in black and white, for all to see. I may have been dreaming, as many of us do, but now I was jolted awake. I was now fully aware that once an idea becomes public, turning back is not an option.

The newsletter editor had said, "More than a runner, Jerry Traylor is an attitude: adventure, curiosity, challenge, dedication and sacrifice bolstered by a wry sense of humor that permits hope for each new day." Was the joke on me? I was not laughing. Could I possibly meet such a challenge? Was I really the person described in that newsletter?

Tom Fenton was determined to help me succeed in spite of myself. He was going to hold me accountable for my vision, and he was not going to let Marietta, Ohio be the only witness to the greatness that he saw within me. Along with the letter praising my Rotary message, Tom enclosed a copy of a letter that he had sent to Senator Bob Dole:

Dear Senator Dole,

A couple of days ago, I saw your reaction (on TV news) to Mr. James Watt's recent unfortunate use of outdated labels. The TV news presented you as a long-time advocate of the handicapped, so if your week has been rendered somewhat gloomy by Mr. Watt, I may be able to brighten things up by sharing with you my admiration and respect for Mr. Jerry Traylor.

The day after Mr. Watt dropped his comments last week, I was introducing Jerry Traylor to our Marietta, Ohio Rotary Club as our luncheon speaker. As you can see by my enclosed letter to Jerry, he held our group spellbound by his story, but even more than that, by his "can-do" resilience and his sense of humor. (I have enclosed a brochure for your perusal.)

I doubt if Mr. Watt's comments hurt anyone but himself; in fact, I bet he gave the handicapped a little extra boost for the 1980s. Jerry is just beginning his career as a speaker and a helper of the handicapped, but I predict someday you'll hear about his work and you'll be proud to be on his team. He's a treasure of a person...and a giver.

Sincerely,

Thomas K. Fenton
Vice President, Fenton Art Glass Company

A treasure? A giver? I gave because I could. For so many years, others gave to me. It is because of their efforts that I can care, that I can contribute.

Ed Cadman, Rotary International President; Mother Hale, founder of Hale House, a home for drug addicted babies; and Jerry Traylor in New York City at the completion of the 1985 Run Across America.

It was seemingly providential that I cast my dream before the Rotarians that day in September 1983. The purpose of Rotary International is to utilize their skills to reach out in service to others. Their motto is, "Service Above Self." In 1954, the year of my birth, the theme chosen by Rotary to capture the year was, "Rotary is Hope in Action." As a child facing incredible difficulties, hope was what I held onto. Now Tom Fenton, with the backing of the Marietta Rotary Club, was prompting me into action. After all, a dream is nothing if we continue to sleep. It is necessary to wake up and put legs to our vision.

Tom Fenton chased the sandman away holding me accountable, as he stayed in close touch throughout the winter. The following spring, we formed a working team of interested Rotarians and began meeting regularly. The group developed a strategic plan and launched the "Trail of New Beginnings Foundation."

Tom was much more than a cheerleader. He spent countless hours writing letters and selling others on the dream. Because of his passion, my purpose never had a chance to fade. In April, Tom took time away from his duties as Vice President of Fenton Art Glass Company to accompany me on a five-day, 75-mile test run from Athens, Ohio to the state capitol in Columbus.

Marietta, Ohio Reception. From left: Tom Fenton; support driver Glen Bartholomew; Jerry; Adrian VanDyk,Carl Clovis and Marshall Kimball.

Rather than just praising me on my goals, Tom Fenton became the wheels beneath my goals. If I stalled, he pushed. When I seemed to lose direction, he prodded. The Trail of New Beginnings was no longer solely my dream. It was a viable working project that would impact countless others.

Caring is a treasure.
Caring offers kudos.
Caring makes headlines.
Caring expresses a vision.
Caring delivers a message.
Caring holds us accountable.
Caring can be a wake-up call.
Caring does not define limits.
Caring might mean taking off work.
Caring means pushing and prodding.
Caring means utilizing what we have.
Caring promotes "service above self."

Points to Ponder

Describe a time when you chose to reach out to another, even though it required a considerable sacrifice on your part. Were your efforts appreciated.

Did you regret this effort later on, or did your sacrifice produce results that made it worthwhile?

Have you ever had someone who cared enough about your growth or project to be willing to regularly meet with you, discuss your vision and hold you accountable? Discuss this experience.

The Trail of New Beginnings

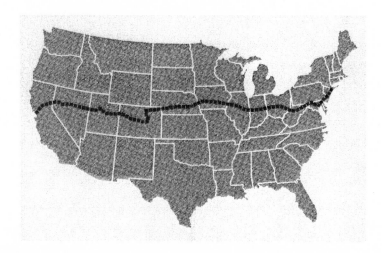

My run across America, designated as *The Trail of New Beginnings,* was designed so that I could give back to others and to celebrate the freedom to walk and run that I had been given. I was able to do this because so many others chose to care and to contribute to helping me realize my potential for life.

As I ran through communities along my route, I gave free talks at schools, non-profit organizations, civic groups and senior facilities. My run was structured to encourage the leaders in each community to identify cultural projects and recreational opportunities for the elderly and the disabled. Rotarians led most local efforts and many grassroots projects were launched. In Pueblo, Colorado, a collection of large-print books for the visually impaired was purchased. In Bloomington, Illinois, recreational equipment was purchased for a senior citizen center. And, in Marietta, Ohio, a nature trail was widened to accommodate wheelchairs.

Throughout my journey, I gave several *Trail of New Beginnings* medallions to remarkably caring achievers who, while dealing with the effects of disabilities or aging, had made positive impacts in their communities.

Untold numbers of individuals supported my efforts. Tom Fenton and Gave Zide, from Marietta, Ohio, facilitated much of the planning and logistics. Randy Greehan from Springfield, Virginia, secured many of the sponsors; Glen Bartholomew joined me as support car driver and all-around assistant on the seven-month journey. Rotarians and others set up local appearances and opened their homes along the route. I am not able to identify all of those who became involved in my efforts, but the following represent a few of the caring people and a few special moments from the 3,528-mile run across America.

Jerry, his sister Janet and mother Marilyn, in Golden Gate Park.

Jerry crosses the Golden Gate Bridge on his crutches.

On February 22, 1985 Barry and Barbara Wishner hosted a send-off party at their home in Woodside, California. Among the guests were many caring individuals that had given so much during their lives.

Dorothy and Bob DeBolt at Woodside, California send-off party.

Dorothy and Bob DeBolt, who over the years have adopted 20 children, 14 of them with disabilities, were at the send-off party. Bob and Dorothy have been featured in scores of national and international newspaper and magazine articles and were the focus of a television documentary, "Who Are the DeBolts?" narrated by Henry Winkler.

Sister Marion Irvine, a Catholic nun who quit smoking and took up running to get in shape in her early 50s, was also there. At age 54, she became the only 50-plus runner to qualify for the Olympic Trials.

On February 24, I had the honor of speaking at the Dominican Sisters School in San Francisco, where Sister Marion is the administrator. The students were fantastic and had enough questions that we could have gone on for several hours. Sister Marion said, "I know you live a life of faith; I will keep you in my prayers each morning and evening." I appreciate her support and concern for my welfare and strength. She is a real inspiration!

ⴔⵝ

Caring means giving back.
Caring means getting in shape.
Caring means providing a home.
Caring means celebrating freedom.
Caring means recognizing achievement.
Caring means identifying and meeting needs.

ⴔⵝ

On March 1, after more than a week on the road, I began running early in the morning, then took a break to speak at the elementary school in Walnut Grove. I resumed running later in the day to complete my daily allotment of nearly 20 miles. When we stopped for the evening, we were touched to find that Marie, the manager of the Rio Vista Sands Motel, and several of her maids had combined their money to treat us to a Mexican dinner. Marie also donated $50 for The Trail of New Beginnings. Rio Vista won my heart as one of the greatest places you could ever be.

On March 8, we stayed at the El Dorado Motel in Placerville, California. I was scheduled to begin the climb into the snow-covered Sierra Nevada Mountains the next day. A teenager knocked on the door and asked for my autograph. A group of high school wrestlers, in town for a tournament, was staying in the adjacent rooms and heard about my journey. They created a steady stream of well-wishers and autograph seekers.

When a child — or anyone, for that matter — asks me to sign an autograph, I pause and teach them that it is a pleasure and real responsibility that comes with the act of signing an autograph. The opportunity does not inflame my ego. Rather, it humbles me. I do not quite understand why God has given me this platform. When I sign an autograph, it is with JOY. It is with the understanding that the recipient is looking up to me — and yet, I am no better than they are. I make every effort to write an entire sentence or paragraph that will long have meaning and give them hope, rather than just penning my name, which should be insignificant. I pretend I am signing my name to a contract, which reads:

"I will continue to live up to all the expectations you have of me...or the high ideals you have for me. I will use this status that you have branded upon me to open new doors, so that I can continue to impact the world in new, unique and positive ways."

On April 27, I was crying! My tears were evidence of the emotion I felt at making the 1,000-mile mark. I was 15 miles from the Colorado border. I thanked the good Lord for allowing me to do this. I thought of my appreciation for the Rotarians...for Glen...for my parents...and for my many friends. It was quite a feeling. I flagged down a passing motorist to celebrate the occasion with us. Others stopped to join in the roadside celebration and to demonstrate a moment of caring.

On Tuesday evening, April 30, as we crossed the Gunnison River heading into Delta, Colorado, we were welcomed by a delegation of some 30 people. Such a reception! Four of them in wheelchairs, one fellow on crutches and five youngsters were all prepared to jog the rest of the day with me.

On May 9, we started between Doylesville and Sargents, Colorado, small towns at the western foot of Monarch Pass, which is on the Continental Divide, 11,312 feet above sea level. About an hour into the day's run, a white Oldsmobile pulled alongside of us. At first, I thought it might be a former college professor of mine, but on closer look I realized it was my father. I could not believe it! I think I jumped two inches into the air. (I cannot jump any higher.) It was just amazing!

My father hopped out of the car and extended his hand as I declared, "Doggone it, Dad, I haven't seen you for over two months. Give me a big hug." I was filled with emotion. It was such a significant event for me because my father had been very athletic and I was, in part, fulfilling a dream to be an athlete of whom he could be proud. I was doing it! I was proving that I was a legitimate athlete, and I was overwhelmed to have my father greet and support me along my journey. He repeatedly drove ahead of me that day and stopped so that he could take pictures. He cared!

What an exciting time! May 16 was the day I would finally run into Pueblo, Colorado, where my parents lived. It had been nearly seven years since I had run in my first race, a three-mile event in the Pueblo City Park. The decision to enter that event as the only runner on crutches has certainly molded my life in a way that few could have imagined.

As I neared the entrance to the planned community of Pueblo West, about eight miles west of the Pueblo city limits, my father greeted me again. He had driven out to check my progress. I told him that I would reach the intersection of Pueblo Boulevard, at the outskirts of Pueblo proper, in about two hours. Closing in on this welcoming party, over 50 people awaited my arrival. But my father was nowhere to be seen, conspicuous in his absence. I later learned that he had gone directly to the hospital as he was worried about chest pains after earlier coming out to greet me. A few weeks later, he had quadruple bypass surgery and spent the next several months in recovery.

⤫

Caring means taking pictures.
Caring means being a role model.
Caring means celebrating success.
Caring means living up to high expectations.
Caring means pooling our resources to help out.

⤫

On July 6, I went to Omaha Children's Hospital, where I interacted with some children one-on-one. During my initial phone call to this facility, the staff had discouraged me from visiting, as there would be so few children there during the July 4 weekend. Remembering all too well the impact of visitors during my own hospitalizations, I was adamant about dropping by. I was able to visit five children. It was not a great number, but their smiles made my journey a whole lot easier. One girl, Jill Neismeyer, was from Creston, Iowa. Her parents were visiting, and her father said that he would greet me upon my arrival there a few days later. Upon arriving in Creston the following week, Jill's father, Marlon, said that I had really brightened her day, not only emotionally, but also in a way that produced positive physical results.

On July 12, I arrived in Osceola, Iowa, and had no speaking commitments until the Rotary dinner at 6:00 p.m. that evening. I was thankful for the lighter schedule. While passing through the small community of Murray, I talked with the Chief of their Police Department, who was struggling with the progressive effects of Muscular Dystrophy. He was doing well, but in recent weeks the city council had wanted to oust him from his position because of his handicap. He asked one of his antagonists if he had seen anything unusual while driving to nearby Creston yesterday. The man answered, "Well, I saw a guy running on crutches." The Chief replied, "Well, he is running across America. You can go out and tell him that he can not run on his crutches, and then, and only then, can you tell me that I cannot work because I am handicapped." He was quite a guy. He had 14 foster children. My efforts had given this man the inspiration to face his distracters.

On July 23, I ran on into Monmouth, Illinois and as I was running through the public square, I heard, "Jerry, Jerry!" I looked around but could not see anyone so I started jogging toward the voices. Five young people came running out of an upstairs apartment and said, "All right, Jerry! Good going! We just saw you on TV a couple of minutes ago." They talked quite a while and one of them asked where I was from. I mentioned that I went to high school in Pueblo, Colorado and one girl proclaimed, "Oh, you're kidding! I'm from Pueblo." It turned out that her brother had played on the basketball team while I was the team's student manager, and her father was David Novak, one of my junior high counselors. That was quite something because her father was a caring educator who had believed in me years earlier.

As I was getting ready for the day on July 24, I received a phone call from a man named Roger Kelly. He explained that his wife Betty, a waitress at a little restaurant just west of Biggsville, Illinois, had met me the day before when she had invited me in for a drink of cool water. Their granddaughter had cerebral palsy. Betty had said, "I certainly wish that my granddaughter could meet you." Roger had called to ask if they could buy us breakfast in the motel restaurant. Their daughter, son-in-law, and even the baby-sitter joined us for breakfast, and they brought little Sarah. It was quite interesting. We all had a good breakfast, and I trust that I was of some inspiration to a youngster who was going through some of the same challenges I had experienced.

On August 10, I continued on along the highway through Lewisville and Straughn, Indiana. When I was running into Straughn, a village of only 256 people, I was incredibly fatigued, having already covered 21 miles. I felt that I would never make it to Columbus, Ohio in the next six days to honor a commitment that I had made. I knew that I should get at least four more miles in, and I was feeling sorry for myself. I was physically beat, exhausted in the heat and almost in tears — with the knowledge that Columbus was still 136 miles away. I was ready to lie down in the road, wondering how much exertion my body could stand.

Through the pain, I heard a little voice say, "Yahoo!" I saw a little girl on her bike go racing by and minutes later, out of a house ran several children. Their yells of, "He's coming, he's coming," and "We love you. Don't stop! Go for it!" echoed in my ears, lifted me, and easily carried me on through Straughn and just short of Aubum. Caring can be so simple and so spontaneous.

On August 27, I was up at 4:30 and running by 5:15 a.m. I was scheduled to arrive in Marietta, Ohio by noon for the Rotary-sponsored parade. As I passed the Barlow Bank, several employees came out to offer encouragement. At just past noon, I ran onto the campus of Washington State Technical College, where I was honored at a lunchtime ceremony and the dedication of a nature trail that had been widened to accommodate wheelchairs. A ramp led up to the path, and was adorned with a sign that read, "Nature Trail for All — Dedicated to making a nature experience for all in commemoration of Jerry Traylor's Run Across America." I was thrilled because the project exemplified why I was running — to prompt others to care and act in service.

Caring can impact others.
Caring is a spontaneous welcome.
Caring means taking time to visit.
Caring means offering accessibility.

❧❧

What a joy it was going across the bridge into West Virginia and the city of Parkersburg on August 28. Parkersburg was the town where I lived when the idea of my run across America started. I had been looking forward to seeing my old friends and neighbors.

Glen took a photo of the symbolic pouring of the by now putrid Pacific Ocean water on the state line. More than 50 runners joined me for those last few blocks and my arrival at the public plaza. My, there were so many people! Could they see my tears? Mayor Pat Pappas, Senator Alan Mollohan and literally hundreds crowded the outdoor ceremony in this burg that I had called home for the last six years. The Parkersburg High School Big Red Band played some rousing patriotic tunes that drew my heart closer to my throat. I had put in six years working as a claims examiner in the savings bond division of the U.S. Treasury Bureau of the Public Debt, in the five-story building that shadowed this plaza. I was touched when Mrs. Henderson, the head of my department, came up to congratulate me on my success. Scores of former fellow employees shared in this joyous and festive reunion.

As I ran through Philadelphia, Pennsylvania on September 30, Randy Greehan, who was helping coordinate my run, strongly advised that I should avoid following my planned route along Highway 40 as it would take me through a rough and rundown section of town. However, I decided to follow the planned route, as I really had nothing but crutches and a pair of running shorts so was not likely to be robbed.

As I ran, I heard a voice calling out, "Hey man, where ya going?" I explained that I was jogging across our country from San Francisco to New York City, hoping to help others who were not as fortunate. I told him that Rotary Clubs were initiating projects in recreation and cultural activities for the elderly and the handicapped, and that my journey was called *The Trail of New Beginnings*. He walked closer, paused, and with a genuine smile on his face, dug into his pocket to pull out a crumpled dollar bill. This rugged looking fellow handed it to me saying, "Ya know, I got a buck in here that ain't doing nothin' tonight." I was impressed by his simple act of caring.

The weeks, months and miles had rolled by. I was finally nearing New York City and would soon dip my weary feet into the cool, soothing salt water of the Atlantic. Like all large undertakings, there had been joyous moments along the trail, but there had also been days that turned into weeks of trudging through scorching heat and driving rain and pushing a body that ached from the top to bottom. But now, the goal was almost in sight. Yet there was one moment lying just ahead that I had not expected.

As I neared New York City, I was startled as a man jumped out from behind a large shrub. What was going on? What did he want? After 3,500 miles along every type of road and community in America, surely I was not going to be attacked. Suddenly, through my frightened eyes, I realized that this man was not there to do any harm. It was my father! Dad had spent five months recovering from that heart attack and had flown to New York to celebrate my accomplishment. Thousands of people along *The Trail of*

New Beginnings had literally, physically cared for me in so many ways. I appreciated every one of them, but my father's appearance at the end of my effort was extra special. Here we were, celebrating each other's triumph over the obstacles and pain of the last seven months. I was so thankful that he was there, along with my Mother, my three sisters, my brother-in-law, Tom Fenton, and several other close friends. I was surrounded by caring — caring that had shaped a life and empowered many a vision.

When we do great things, people want to be part of our journey. All of us, regardless of what we possess, no matter what our status, want to care. I have learned that if you and I are passionate about a cause, others will support us. If I am ever in danger of starving, all I will have to do is reach out in service to others and those who see my mission will embrace it and take care of me.

After seven months and 3,528 weary miles, the sign says it all!

Jerry Traylor greeting onlookers at a parade in New York City, two days
after the completion of his transcontinental run.

I believe in the goodness of people. This was evidenced in
hundreds of simple acts of caring as I trekked across this
wonderful country, and it has been a critical part of my
entire life. The success I have experienced is a result of the
goodness of others who stepped forward to help me from the
day of my birth until the present. I will continue to fulfill my
goals with the caring assistance of many more people —
and, I hope that I will always give far more to others than I
receive along my lifelong *Trail of New Beginnings*.

Project Jerry: Helping Kids Be Overcomers

Jerry Traylor spends every waking hour overcoming......

Born with cerebral palsy, moving from a body cast to a wheelchair to crutches, who would have thought it possible? Only Jerry Traylor. Jerry believed he could run across America. Seven months and 3,528 miles later he accomplished his goal. Now Jerry spends his life helping young people overcome the handicaps of negative peer pressure and poor self image—an overcomer, helping others overcome.

In addition to a national speaking tour, Jerry serves on staff with Youth Leadership Council conducting elementary and high school assembly programs about overcoming, especially as it relates to teen issues of drugs, alcohol and sexuality. Jerry's message to kids is "You can be an overcomer. You can do what is right, no matter how hard it seems."

Jerry's message of faith, courage and determination has been heard by children and youth in schools nationwide. He tells how God has enabled him to fight through his apparent limitations and achieve what would seem impossible for someone who cannot walk without aid of crutches. Youth Leadership Council is privileged to have Jerry spearheading assembly programs in area schools. He makes a difference in the lives of young people.

Caring means embracing a mission.
Caring is a tearful, touching reunion.
Caring is hearing and feeling a patriotic tune.
Caring means reaching for a crumpled dollar bill.

Points to Ponder

Have you ever identified a need in your community and taken the initiative to spearhead an effort to meet the need? Describe your efforts. What is a concern which you can identify with and how might you get involved or empower others to get involved?

In this chapter, I introduce you to Bob and Dorothy DeBolt who adopted an incredible number of children, many with special needs. Who has been the most caring person that you have personally known? Talk about him or her, and also discuss the most powerful demonstration of caring that you have ever witnessed, whether or not you were the recipient.

Describe a time when you chose to care where in hindsight you were able to see that your efforts produced positive results.

Do you typically empower others in their quest, or are you likely to be a doubting Thomas who says it can't be done? Is it possible to change to be more supportive?

Name a time when you were struggling and someone came along at seemingly just the right time with a caring gesture or kind word that seemed to take away your difficulty.

The Window Pain

As I stood in the crowded mall, my breathing quickened and a lump rose in my throat as the lean figure approached. It had been twenty years since our last meeting, and the memories were not always pleasant. His orders had mandated my transfer to an institution 240 miles from my family. My parents were allowed to visit, but they were able to do so only every two weeks or so.

I would stand at the window as they were leaving, tears flooding down my cheeks. Looking down, I could see my three sisters gazing up at the window as I stood silently framed in the pain of the moment. My sisters were not allowed into the institution and as my family walked away, I felt terribly, excruciatingly alone.

The squirrels ran about the lawn and among the massive oaks taunting me with their playfulness. Why did they have such freedom? Why? Why did they have freedom while I was confined for more than eleven months at one stretch?

The physical pain was also nearly unbearable at times. Some people would grimace at what could be labeled torture. My bones were broken, my limbs were twisted, and deep incisions were inflicted on my body. During each parental visit, I begged my parents to take me home. I had done nothing wrong. I didn't deserve this. Life wasn't fair, and yet, the smile broke through. The smile was always there on my five-year-old face.

My mind suddenly jumped back to the present. This man with graying hair reached out his hand. Rather than grimacing as I might have done nearly two decades ago, my ready smile greeted Dr. Howard Mitchell. Although it was his orders that had sent me to my lonely hospital confinement, it was Dr. Mitchell's caring hands that had set me free.

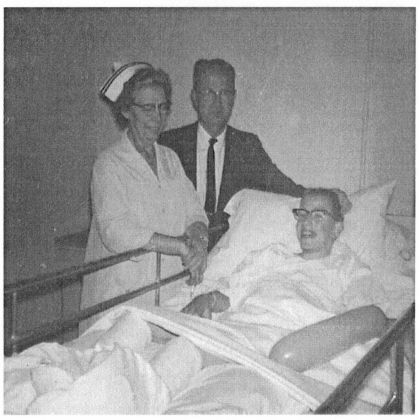

Jerry at age 12 during recovery from yet another surgery, with a nurse and Doctor Howard Mitchell.

My transcontinental run was over halfway complete as I greeted Dr. Mitchell at Lawlor's Sporting Goods store at Gateway Mall in Lincoln, Nebraska. I had last seen Dr. Mitchell as a twelve-year-old when he released me from his care following my father's work transfer to Colorado. Dr. Mitchell's surgical expertise through numerous corrective orthopedic operations had shaped my legs and sculpted a platform for my rapidly growing body. His caring touch had made mobility and independence possible for me. Now, he greeted me along with Nina Johnson, a former nurse. Their smiles brightened the room as they looked in awe at the transformation. The child who had once struggled to cross the room in waist-high metal braces was now crossing the United States on crutches and celebrating the freedom that they had helped give him.

Dr. Mitchell and I had a chance to sit down for a brief visit. He told me that he was amazed that I had done so well. He shared his love of bicycling, which he did nearly every day to stay in shape. I must say that his physique was incredible for someone in his early 70s.

Several years later, I received a letter from Florence Mitchell stating that her husband had passed away. As Dr. Mitchell was making his daily 25-mile bicycle trip along the MoPac Trail in Lincoln, a car struck him. His life ended at the age of 87, while on the trail he loved. Our paths had crossed on the trail of life, and my future was made so much better by his caring.

In her touching letter, Mrs. Mitchell told of the joy her husband felt when I called him during my cross-country journey — when I took the time to locate and thank him. She said he was immensely proud to stand beside me in that mall. Dr. Mitchell, because of you, I can run, and run I continue to do — down that joyful trail of life. Thank you!

Footnote: While running across America on crutches, I was often billed as a hero. Individuals of all ages lauded me for what I was able to accomplish. To many, I was "achieving the impossible" in spite of my limitations. Ironically, the real heroes were many of those very people who thought that I was superhuman. It was those caring individuals who made my journey possible.

In Memory of Dr. Howard E. Mitchell

Great Plains Trails Network Newsletter, September, 1999
By Beth Thacker, GPTN Editor

Almost daily, rain or shine, Dr. Howard Mitchell would strap on his bike helmet, wheel his bike out, and head for the MoPac Trail from his home on North 56th Street. He would ride to Eagle for tea and rolls at Grandmother's Cafe, often being joined by his buddies John, Jim and Cornie. The ride home meant a 25-mile round-trip. For many of us, just the thought of a 25-mile daily bicycle ride seems daunting. For Howard, it was nothing out of the ordinary, in spite of the fact that he was 87 years old. In fact, Howard's last moments were on the trail he loved, when, this summer, he was struck and killed by a car while crossing A Street near 98th. The northbound stop sign had been stolen over the weekend, and Howard apparently didn't see the car as he entered the intersection.

The MoPac Trail was a big part of Howard Mitchell's life. He loved to watch the sun rise from the trail. In fact, he saw many sunrises as he made the almost daily 25-mile bicycle ride to Eagle and back over the past 6 years. Howard spent so much time on the MoPac that it became a family joke that, when his two sons came to town to visit, the one place they could find him for sure was pedaling between Lincoln and Eagle on the MoPac. The trail meant so much to him that friends and family have donated more than $1,000 to it in his memory.

The Mitchells, Howard and Florence, came to Lincoln more than 50 years ago, planning to stay only 6 months while Howard completed a temporary position in orthopedic medicine. They stayed a bit longer than that, raising two boys and becoming very involved in the medical community.

Dr. Mitchell was a former director for the Nebraska Orthopedic Hospital in Lincoln. He also had a private practice and was noted for helping children with cerebral palsy. In the mid-1980s the Nebraska Medical Association honored him for 50 years of service.

The once familiar figure, pedaling to and from Eagle, will be missed by many. But what a legacy of health and fitness he leaves for those of us who will continue to enjoy the seasons on the MoPac.

Caring helps us reconnect.
Caring can make physical pain bearable.
Caring can reach beyond our earthly existence.
Caring can be accompanied by difficult emotions.
Caring individuals will likely live a productive life.

Points to Ponder

I obviously cringed every time that I was scheduled to visit my doctor. As a child I did not realize that struggles were necessary to facilitate my future potential. Name someone from your childhood with whom you struggled as he or she worked to mold you for the future, possibly an educator who seemed to pick on you, parents who expected too much, etc.

Discuss how their efforts did, in fact, produce results.

If applicable, tell about a time that you as an adult have been able to reconnect with one of these caring individuals. What was it like?

A Captive Audience

I had mixed feelings about addressing such a group. I knew that it would be a captive audience, however I also felt shivers of anxiety as I walked through the gate and heard the harsh sound of metal closing heavily behind me.

As I walked into the chapel where this program was to take place, my eyes met those of a wheelchair-bound man who appeared to be in his sixties, sitting in the front row. I told the chaplain that I had an eerie feeling that I had seen this individual before.

Part of the program I presented that day detailed the early years of my life, showing scenes of my childhood when I was confined to a series of body casts and braces. During the question and answer period following my talk, the man I had seen earlier, in a very feeble voice not much more than a whisper, asked if I had been in the nearby Nebraska Orthopedic Hospital back in 1960.

I found myself speechless and unable to respond immediately to his question. It became obvious that we recognized each other from a time and place some 33 years earlier. Jim Fish had been an inmate at the Nebraska state prison back in 1960. In an escape attempt, he had broken his back while attempting to jump to freedom from the top of the prison wall. Following back surgery, this fellow had been placed in the same hospital where I was being treated.

I remembered this man, who even in his thirties had been slightly balding. From my perspective as a six-year-old, this caring man, so ready with a friendly word, had been someone that I loved to see in that lonely hospital ward. In my young, naïve mind, this man had an important purpose.

When Jim came rolling down the hall, we kids gathered close to him, wanting to be near someone who outwardly spread so much cheer. We knew that the pouch in the back of his wheelchair was brimming with comic books that he lovingly shared with all of us.

My six-year-old mind and the caring spirit of this gentle man would never have allowed me to believe the truth. Three years earlier, Jim Fish had shot a state trooper to death and therefore would reside in the nearby Nebraska State Penitentiary until his dying day.

It was a miracle that we were brought together again. This was even more apparent when, two weeks after my presentation at the penitentiary, I received a letter from Fritzie Kurtzer, one of my mother's cousins who lived in Lincoln. Inside Fritzie's letter I found a newspaper clipping from the *Lincoln Star Journal.* It was an obituary stating that Jim had passed away at the age of 67, due to complications from Parkinson's disease. It was only as I read this news that I came to know Jim's full story.

Jim Fish had been careless. Jim paid dearly for his mistakes in that state penitentiary. Jim Fish, however, still chose to care right where he was. With laughter and love, his caring brightened a hospital ward of desperate kids.

Caring captivates.
Caring can be a miracle.
Caring can spread cheer.
Caring can be your escape.
Caring can give you purpose.
Caring can leave you speechless.
Caring can bring laughter and love.
Caring can send shivers down your spine.
Caring can bring you in touch with the past.
Caring is the life sentence we should all face.

Points to Ponder

In this story, I remember Jim's caring but I knew nothing about his violent past. Have you ever experienced or witnessed a caring act by someone who had a different reputation?

Did this observation change the way you felt about that person in future encounters?

Hall of Fame

The following was written as my acceptance speech, to be read at my induction into the *Pueblo Sports Hall of Fame*. I had missed this honor in my former home town because of a prior commitment to attend the Victory Award ceremony which took place in Washington, D.C. that same weekend.

To my fellow inductees, friends and family:

As a student at South High School, I used to idolize all of my peers who nabbed the passes for touchdowns, fired up a two-pointer from just inside the key, or rounded second base after hitting a line drive into left field.

There were times when I felt inadequate, and in some ways, cheated. I was just a skinny little guy who was forced to lean on two metal sticks for support. I wanted so desperately to be normal.

As a sophomore at South, Bert Stjernholm and Rocky Sisneros, football co-captains, invited me to lead cheers during Spirit Week and to sit on the team bench for the game. This was a simple gesture, but possibly life-changing. Bert and Rocky appreciated the spirit I demonstrated. They believed in me!

It's miraculous. When someone believes in you, you start to believe in yourself. You can move from conceiving — to believing — to achieving.

My opportunities for growth and achievement would have been impossible in ancient Greece. Even well known philosophers such as Aristotle, Plato and Socrates believed in the Law of Exposure, which stated that any person of less than physical perfection would be left on the mountainside to perish.

Rather than perish, I survived — no, I actually prevailed. Today, I feel fortunate to have my crutches. As I look back on my life, I am thankful for the opportunities that have come my way. I no longer desire to be normal. Normalcy is a standard that so many seek, but I now realize that we can go above and beyond "normal."

It humbles me to accept this honor — to have a chance to be a role model. I am absolutely bewildered when I remember the daily struggles that I experienced on my 3,500-mile run across America. It astounds me to think that such a dream could have been fulfilled. Without the great expectations others had for me, I would not even have begun such a journey.

As a six-year-old, I remember lying in a hospital bed following one of many painful operations, and wondering, "Why, why, why did I have to face such struggles?" Then as I awakened from ether-induced sleep, I felt the grip of my mother's hand on mine. "Jerry, one of these days things will be better," she said. My mother gave me hope and taught me patience.

While trying to cope with the unkind remarks of others, I often felt like crying. The pain of being different, of not being able to keep up, was harsh.

Today, having climbed Pikes Peak to 14,110 feet, having parachuted from 12,500 feet, experienced the thrill of skiing, the camaraderie of golf and bowling leagues, and the enormity of a coast-to-coast run, I truly feel that my current mission is the most important. My mission is to teach our youth to believe in themselves; to make positive choices for fulfilling futures; to find a mission, a purpose, an opportunity to touch and change the world, one step at a time.

Running 3,500 miles is a long journey. Seven and a half months is a long time, but I feel that it was a small price to *pay. That period of time was only 1/100th of my expected lifespan, and I am thankful for each new step.*

My induction into the Greater Pueblo Sports Association Hall of Fame is certainly a special honor. It is also an obligation on my part to live up to new levels of service, to go forward to give to others a portion of what has been given to me.

With great love, joy and the Lord's blessings, I thank you for the continued support. Thank you.

Caring can change a life.
Caring allows us to cope.
Caring is a pillar of support.
Caring means believing in others.
Caring means being a cheerleader.
Caring allows us to go beyond normalcy.
Caring is something we get through Christ.
Caring can carry us forward on our journeys.
Caring unconditionally is not a part of all cultures.
Caring may be the catalyst that leads to greatness.

Points to Ponder

Have you ever been valued as a member of a team, athletically or otherwise, even though you would never become a star?

Have you ever known a renowned athlete or "cool" individual who was willing to spend his or her social capital interacting with ordinary people? If so, did this person use the enhanced visibility to make a positive difference rather than just saying, "Look at me?" Talk about this.

If you were to be inducted into a 'Hall of Fame,' for what would it be? Does this match the legacy that you might want to leave?

A Victory Celebration

In September 1991, Carol Wells, a social worker in the Tampa, Florida, school system, told me about the nomination form for the national Victory Awards that had come across her desk. The honor was designated to recognize individuals who had shown courage and strength in the face of adversity.

Carol had been a dear friend since October 1988 when I met her following a presentation I gave to a group of educators in Florida. Carol's touching story could fill a book. Her son Aaron had been taken from this world just a year and a half earlier at the tender age of five because of haemophilus meningitis. Carol had grieved deeply as any mother would, but had made Aaron's short life count as she led a crusade to educate parents about a vaccine that could have saved her son. My message deeply touched and encouraged her to continue her mission.

A few weeks later, I excitedly called Carol to tell her that I had heard from Maggie Fogel, a member of the planning committee for the Victory Award ceremony in Washington, D.C. Maggie had called to congratulate me on my selection as the Ohio state recipient. She asked if I had heard from the Governor's office. When I said no, she said that the intent of the phone call was merely to congratulate me, not to inform me of the honor. She said the details would follow in the mail.

Soon after, I excitedly read the details of the Victory Award celebration scheduled for mid-November. So much was planned! On Monday, November 19, the honorees were even scheduled to have tea with First Lady Barbara Bush in the White House Rose Garden. As I looked at my calendar, I realized that I had a prior commitment on that very day. I was scheduled to address about 600 teens at a student council conference in Tennessee.

After a very brief period of contemplation, I called Maggie to tell her that I would come to Washington, D.C. to accept my Victory Award, but that I would be unavailable to attend the Rose Garden Tea. Maggie suggested that I cancel the engagement in Tennessee because this was a once-in-a-lifetime opportunity. She thought the student council could surely find another speaker. I agreed that would be possible, but I had always tried to do the right thing. I was not going to tell 600 teenagers that there was something more important than speaking to them. This conference keynote address had been on my calendar for over a year, and I planned to be there.

Continental Airlines provided two complimentary round trip tickets for each state recipient of the Victory Awards. Without hesitation, I decided to invite Carol Wells to come from Florida to Washington for the awards ceremony because she had been so supportive of my activities. I also called my mother in Colorado, because the honor was a victory and a tribute to my parents as well as to me.

As my mother answered the phone, I asked if she could take a couple of days off work about a month later. She emphatically told me that there was no way she could possibly get more time off, as she was already scheduled to be off at Christmas time. I said, "Well, Mother, Mrs. Bush will be disappointed that you will not be able to visit her at the White House."

I am pretty sure my mother was in tears as she haltingly replied, "Oh, Jerry! Oh, Jerry, I can't believe it!" She told me that she would talk to her supervisor to see if she could take some personal time beyond her scheduled vacation.

Since my parents were divorced, I made another call to my father. Although he was excited about the honor, he ultimately chose to represent me at the Greater Pueblo, Colorado Sports Hall of Fame where I was slated for induction that very same week.

With growing excitement, I met my mother and Carol Wells at National Airport in Washington. We stayed at the infamous Watergate Hotel for two nights, and on Sunday, took a bus to the Kuwaiti Cultural Center where His Excellency Shaikh Saud Nasir Al-Sabah, the Ambassador of Kuwait, hosted an evening reception. The next day, we attended a luncheon at the National Rehabilitation Hospital where we mingled with actors Leslie Nielsen and William Christopher, who starred in the hit television series *M.A.S.H.* One-armed professional baseball pitcher Jim Abbott and others were also present.

My mother, Marilyn Traylor, His Excellency Shaikh Saud Nasir Al-Sabah, the Ambassador of Kuwait, Carol Wells and me.

The following Monday evening, Mother, Carol and I dressed to the nines for a gala black-tie ceremony at the Kennedy Center for the Performing Arts. Actor Cliff Robertson was the emcee for the program, which featured many special guests, including the state-level Victory Award winners. Arnold Schwarzenegger, Crystal Gayle, Phylicia Rashad, and President H.W. and Mrs. Bush were in attendance. National Victory Awards went to singer Gloria Estefan, comedian Norm Crosby, actor Sandy Duncan and others.

When the celebration ended shortly after midnight, Mark Braxton, a friend of Maggie Fogel's, drove me to Knoxville while I slept. There were no flights leaving late that night, and I was so exhausted that I did not dare risk making the drive by myself. We arrived two hours before my speech to the student council. About the time I began my presentation, my mother and Carol were sipping tea with Barbara Bush.

While in Washington, I had somehow lost my wallet. It contained a substantial amount of money, my identification and credit cards. On the day before Thanksgiving, I checked with my office to see if there were any messages that I should return. The answering service informed me of an unexpected call from the Metropolitan Police Department in Washington, D.C. My fingers trembled as I dialed the number and asked to speak to Officer Thompson. Moments later, I felt like dancing on the rooftops when he informed me that someone had found my wallet and turned it in with all of the money and cards intact.

We enjoyed the thrill of the celebrity-laden celebration in Washington, but in addition to the Victory Award, which now adorned the wall of my office, we celebrated other victories that were far more meaningful. Carol Wells had turned the tragic death of her son into motivation for her own positive project, and she was helping others as never before. I had made the right decision to honor my commitment to speak to 600 young people instead of canceling on them at the last minute. And an unknown person had proven that people do care about the welfare of others by passing up an opportunity to keep several hundred dollars when he turned the lost wallet into the police. This simple, caring act of honesty once again confirmed the goodness of the human spirit.

My upcoming Thanksgiving was bound to be a great one.

Caring is celebrating victory.
Caring sees opportunity in distress.
Caring means dressing to-the-nines.
Caring means keeping a commitment.
Caring means embarking on a crusade.
Caring is sipping tea in the Rose Garden.
Caring means returning what is not yours.
Caring is recognizing greatness in everyday heroes.

135

Points to Ponder

Have you ever been able to turn a difficult situation, possibly even a tragedy, into an opportunity to serve others? Explain.

Discuss a time when you made a commitment, only to be faced with another, possibly more enticing, opportunity. Did you keep your word and follow through with your original commitment?

Whether you did or not, how did your decision make you feel? If you passed up a "better" opportunity, did you feel cheated?

A Mother's Love

April Fool's Day was coming soon. I looked forward to it, as this day always brought many surprises in our home. When I was growing up, my mother always seemed to have a favorite trick she would play on my three sisters and me. Usually, we sat at the kitchen table and scarfed down a quick bowl of cereal and a glass of juice before heading out the door for a brisk walk to school. Invariably, the glasses of grape juice that sat on our placemats on this particular day turned out to be glasses of water with purple food coloring.

I harbor so many memories of a mother who orchestrated a true celebration of life through the little things she did. These memories are so very precious.

This April Fool's Day would be different. It was close to noon a few days before April Fool's Day when my sister Judy called me to say that my mother was in the hospital. The urgency in my sister's voice assured me that this was no early April Fool's Day prank. My sister said that my mother had been on an outing with a family friend. Apparently, as our friend Jim returned to his lane after passing a truck on the highway, he lost control of the vehicle. The car rolled over two times and skidded on its top another hundred feet before crashing into a barrier. The vehicle was destroyed. Jim was not seriously injured and assisted my mother as she tried to crawl out of the car.

First-responder caregivers arrived on the scene almost immediately, but it was 45 minutes before an ambulance arrived to transport my mother to St. Mary Corwin Hospital in Pueblo, some thirty miles away.

By the time my sister had called me, our mother had already reached the intensive-care unit, but details about her injuries were scarce. My other sisters and I, who all lived in Phoenix, waited anxiously for another call from Judy with more information.

When the word finally came, we learned how lucky my mother was even to be alive. A few days later, the doctor informed us that the prognosis of surgery could not even be assessed. We learned that very few patients even survive such severe injuries. This injury was the same that had paralyzed actor Christopher Reeve; surgery would be extremely high risk.

Remarkably, mother's surgery was successful. She then faced months of healing, 24-hour care, and finally, therapy. It was impossible for her to do even the simplest things. Mother struggled with the fact that all she could do was lie stationery with a metal brace and rods stabilizing her neck and head to prevent movement. Aides provided her most basic care. For so many years, Mother had been the caregiver for her family and many others. Now, everything was reversed.

About a month after the accident, my sister Janet visited Mother and played an audiotape of a recent appearance I had made on a popular national radio program. As the tape ended, Mother openly wept and cried out, "I can't believe it. He was supposed to die. He was supposed to die. Thank God, he lived!" My mother's great compassion and love for me still overwhelms me. But now, it was my turn to comfort and inspire her during the long recovery.

Following 18 months of surgeries and extensive therapy, Mother gradually resumed a fairly normal life. She has continued to make remarkable progress. Today, she cares and gives continually. Almost every week she sends 10 to 20 personal letters and cards to encourage others, and regularly takes groceries and good cheer to an elderly lady. She insists on taking friends to lunch, and encourages folks to stop and stay overnight with her anytime they are near her home in Pueblo. Mother says that facing the prospect of living the rest of her life without mobility and in constant pain taught her how wonderful it is to be healthy and able to give to others.

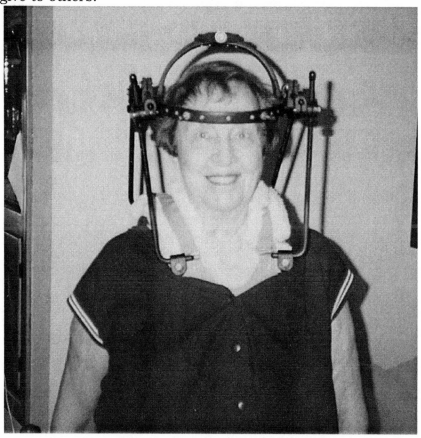

My mother, Marilyn Traylor, wore a metal halo and a grateful smile after surviving a broken neck and long recovery.

Obviously, I love and appreciate my mother beyond measure. THANK GOD SHE LIVED!

Caring offers renewed life.
Caring can be orchestrated.
Caring means taking action.
Caring puts out the welcome mat.
Caring means giving to the caregiver.
Caring opportunities grow during difficulties.
Caring for others is a role we will all play at times.
Caring for others is a way to voice our thanksgiving.

Points to Ponder

As you have read in this story, my mother was accustomed to being the caregiver and struggled when forced to be on the receiving end. Which role have you played most often?

Discuss a time when you had to take the opposite role.

How did it feel to give when you typically receive?

How did it feel when others were addressing your needs when you were used to catering to others?

Did the caring that others gave you make you a more caring person?

The Caring Communicator

Ralph Bloss loved to talk. He loved to communicate. He had a way of speaking that was uniquely Ralph, and there were many sayings he used so often that they became known to his friends and associates as "Ralphisms." For example, "Everything you do communicates something" was a favorite Ralphism.

I first met Ralph Bloss following my speech at a sales meeting for Ohio Steamway, a carpet-cleaning organization. John Maucieri motioned for me and said, "I want to introduce you to Ralph Bloss, President of Steamway International out of Denver, Colorado." As I shook Ralph's hand, I said, "Mr. Bloss, I am scheduled to fly to Colorado next week. I am going to get a rental car and travel to Frisco where I will speak at an elementary school, then I am going to drive down to Pueblo and visit my parents for Easter." Ralph looked me square in the eyes and declared, "No, you're not!"

No, I'm not? What was Ralph communicating? How could he dictate what I was or was not going to do? Since it was my first time to meet Ralph — in fact, the first few seconds that I had ever been in his presence — I was slightly taken aback by his directness. I could have judged him to be rude and arrogant, but I would have been so very wrong.

Ralph continued, "You are not going to get a rental car. I will meet you at Denver International Airport in our company car, you drop me back by our office and take the car as long as you need it." From that very first moment, Ralph communicated caring, and caring is all I ever heard from him in the 13 years he was a part of my life.

Ralph made sure that I was utilized as a speaker in the carpet cleaning and restoration industry. Ralph, his wife Anjunell and their three children, Doyle, Greg and Sharolyn, became family to me. When my father passed away, Ralph became the closest thing to a father that I had.

I smiled every time Ralph answered my phone calls. His cheerful voice greeted me with, "Good morning, better looking than I am and a whole lot younger. To what do I owe this call from a man of such distinction, character and personality?" Ralph made everyone look good and visits with him never grew old.

Ralph always ended each phone call by saying, "I love you. If I can ever help you out be sure and call me. If anyone ever needs a reference to use you as a speaker, please have him call me. You are the best!"

Ralph Bloss empowered many in his life.

"Someone who encourages us to do our best and to be our best is most often the person who ends up as our most honored friend and trusted mentor," was another favorite Ralphism. It proved true to me.

Ralph started his business in 1982, but he had been in sales since the early 1930s when his father became ill and was unable to work. During those Great Depression days, nine-year-old Ralph sold magazines and did whatever he could to put food on the table.

Another Ralphism, from a 1958 speech, embodied his business philosophy. "If your road to success is built on the backs of others, you will eventually come to a hill too high. If your road to success is built by giving others a boost, they will be there to boost you up the highest hill."

Ralph cared about all of his business acquaintances, clients and competitors alike. It was not always easy, but even when he had to take a loss, Ralph was committed to doing the right thing. Ralph declared, and demonstrated, "If you don't love your customers, go do something else."

We recently lost Ralph. In the touching memorial service, the minister shared another Ralphism: "'In the business world, you don't just make promises. You either do or you don't do what you say.'" Ralph Bloss lived this way. The reason Ralph gave so much was because he knew the Lord's love and the responsibility to use the gifts that he had been given."

Doyle, Ralph's oldest son, read the following tribute at Ralph's memorial service:

> *"I know that many who have lost a loved one often find comfort in a small memento that reminds them of their loved one, or something that was given to them by that loved one. The day after Dad died, I woke up and decided that I needed to identify something that he had given to me or maybe something that he had picked up along the way that meant a lot to him. I started thinking about what that thing might be. Within*

minutes I was frustrated and almost angry with myself because I could not think of anything. I could not think of one thing that meant a lot to Dad. It was only adding to my sadness.

Then, like a bolt of lightning from heaven, the truth came over me. My Dad did not value things. He did not have a hobby. He did not collect or cherish things. His life, his value, was found in his relationships with people and his relationship with God. Whether it be towards his wife or his children or one of his grandchildren, he found his greatest joy in loving them. He was like a constant cruise director, making sure everyone had plenty to eat, and was being properly entertained. He found happiness in helping and nurturing a young couple with a new carpet cleaning business and taking them under his wings. He loved to help grow and develop churches and Christian-based organizations. I was Dad's "thing." You were Dad's "thing." Dad's "thing" was almost every person he ever encountered.

I realized at that point what my memento was, what my reminder would be. It is you, the friends, family, brothers and sisters in Christ, customers, co-workers, employees, business associates, and even competitors. The people he touched were the mementos that he left for us; the changed lives. The joy he brought.

It was in your success, joy, happiness and satisfaction that my Dad found his greatest joy. It is as you continue to pursue success, by the happy things that happen in your life, by you developing your faith in the Creator and God who loves you so much, by the things Dad taught you to help you along the way. It is all of you. You are the mementos that Dad left for us. Thank you for being those important mementos."

I recall many visits to the Bloss family cabin along Big Thompson River in Estes Park, Colorado. It seems that the door was open to everyone. It was a perfect place to get away and to reflect on life. Along Highway 34 at the entrance to that cozy respite was a wooden sign inscribed with the words of Christ as read in Matthew 7:24 – 25:

"Therefore, everyone who hears these words of mine and puts them into practice is like a wise man who built his house

on the rock. The rain came down, the streams rose, and the winds blew and beat against that house, yet it did not fall, because it had its foundation on the rock."

Ralph knew upon what to build his life's foundation. Ralph lived with the belief that Christ was first, others were second, and self came last.

During Ralph's funeral service, his son Greg reflected:

> *During our Easter service on Sunday, my oldest son Marcus saw a short movie where the artist showed Jesus ascending to heaven with wings like an angel. My son Marcus asked, "Dad, is Granddad an angel?" I said, "Sure son, you can bet that he is." Later that night Marcus heard his little brother, Nicholas say, "Granddad can fly now!"*

Ralph Bloss taught us to fly. He gave us wings. Everything he did communicated caring.

Caring can be direct.
Caring gives unexpectedly.
Caring means expressing love.
Caring is like an honored friend.
Caring greets others with cheer.
Caring should not be judgmental.
Caring should be communicated.
Caring means doing the right thing.
Caring means giving others a boost.
Caring validates the good of others.
Caring encourages others to do their best.

Points to Ponder

Have you ever had a friend who continually brightened your day if you had contact with him or her? Talk about this individual.

Do you tend to greet others so that their day is made better for having been in your presence?

Megan Crow, a senior at Arnold High School in Nebraska, wrote this poem after hearing Jerry speak at a leadership camp.

Dare to Care

Thousands of dollars given
To construct a building of time
Millions of people in the crowd
To hear a singer in her prime

Hours of lives dedicated
To produce a glorious change
Years of research just completed
To be recognized by name

All of this, and more, it's great
Seems to sit on angels' wings
But sometimes what mean more in life
Are many of the smaller things

One single hug from that nurse
To get through a night of pain
A few tears cried by a little girl
Who has nothing much to gain

Nights of forever spent wondering
To crawl beside Mom and lie wide awake
Years of friends' friendly laughter
To help keep promises that they make

Steps so small that whispers arise
But can't be heard over cheering fans
Falls so hard that fingers point
But can't be seen behind dozens of helping hands

Life is a winding journey
And can lead all of us astray
Others are there all along
And can pull us different ways

Some ways lead to golden roads
The others, probably dead ends
Get away from the hollow people
Keep the others – they make good friends

After all is said and done
To stay true to ourselves is the dare
But the most difficult challenge I give you
Is to always live fully, yet give great care

Because tears mean more than money
And hugs last longer than fame
Those in our lives best-remembered
Don't end up with well-known names

The little acts are what mean so much
And keep us going day-to-day
So try all the time with all your might
To be someone who leads to the golden way

7-28-05
Dedicated to Jerry Traylor and all of the others who have
changed my life – I'll never forget you. –mc

Caring Dedication

Now that you have finished reading these essays of caring, I imagine that you more fully understand the reason I have been able to achieve a great deal even though I was physically blessed with less than many. From an early age, I have been surrounded by caring individuals who empowered me in my daily activities. I dedicate this work to the most caring person of all — my mother, Marilyn Traylor. She is such a powerful example of what it really means to care, to serve, to love.

Jerry's mom, Marilyn Traylor, in a reflective moment in Estes Park, Colorado.

Thankfully, my own daughter, Sarah Traylor, has continued this mission of caring. I am so proud of her involvement in school activities and her willingness to embrace other kids who may not be the most popular. Sarah inspires me with her attitude. I feel sure that she will succeed in many ways as she ventures forward in her life journey.

My daughter, Sarah, is as smart and caring as she is beautiful!

More Points to Ponder

After reading the stories in this book of how others have assisted me along life's journey, you may find value in initiating some discussion on the importance of caring in a significant life. I believe that all of us will be the recipient of caring on occasion, and I also believe that each of us, regardless of our situation, can help others. A person doesn't have to be wealthy, or highly educated, or physically beautiful or have any special skills to care about others.

Following are more general questions and issues that will challenge you and help you reflect on what caring has meant in your life, and how you can grow in your attitude of caring.

This document will help facilitate discussion in many venues, whether at school, in a book club, in a small group at church, in a family setting or even in the workplace.

We can all *Live**CARE**fully.*

What in your background has instilled the value of caring in your life?

When in your life were you most in need of caring? Did anyone know? How did you convey the need to those who might help?

When someone did a caring act for you, did it change your long term relationship with that person? How did you express your appreciation?

Has there been a time when you reached out in caring for another person, even though you did not particularly like or respect the individual in need of assistance?

Have you ever had to show caring in a manner that was not appreciated, i.e., intervention in an abusive or self-destructive situation?

If your efforts in caring are not appreciated, do you continue to offer support in the future?

Does the act of caring about others ever become automatic, or do you have to consciously seek opportunities?

Is there any way to instill the value of caring in others?

How can we take steps to make sure we care?

Corporate Programs

Jerry Traylor offers personal motivation beyond that of speakers famed for their athletic and business achievements. Jerry's message is "real world." It hits home with audiences who can apreciate the value of pushing beyond limitations rather than merely exploiting natural talent.

Some would claim that Jerry Traylor is, in his own right, a sports hero. He has climbed to the top of Pikes Peak (14,110 feet) three times, run 3,528 miles across America from San Francisco to New York, and has competed in 35 marathons...all on crutches. In addition, he has parachuted from 12,500 feet.

However, Jerry's message is not about overcoming a handicap caused by cerebral palsy. What Jerry does talk about is the remarkable contribution all of us can make in our workplace and in our society. Jerry challenges his audiences, creating a feeling, a new way ot thinking that empowers listeners to action, and that prompts them to do whatever it takes to meet the needs of each customer and provide a quality product or service. Jerry's humor and heart leave an indelible impact on audiences as he inspires each person toward achievement of difficult goals.

Over the past 29 years Jerry Traylor has inspired over one million individuals in 48 states and abroad, ranging from industry giants like IBM and DuPont to the smallest partnership. In addition, he speaks at many conferences focusing on issues such as Sales, Customer Service and Quality Assurance.

These comments are from just a few of Jerry's customers:

"Jerry, I have heard many incredible speakers, but I have never seen anyone captivate the audience like you did. When we weren't laughing, you had us crying; and you left us inspired and motivated. You sure know how to make an educational chairman a hero. Thanks!"
- Val M. Ross, Education Chairman, Western Assn. of College Bookstores

"What can I say? The standing ovation said it all. You were fantastic, just as I knew you would be. You said many times how privileged you felt to live in the United States and to be alive. Let me say how privileged I feel to have been able to get to know you and share your message with my co-workers. They loved you."
- Carolyn A. Landry, Secretary of the State Director, Vermont - Farmers Home Administration

"The purpose of our meeting was to announce a new program to our vendors. We wanted a speech that was strong in commitment, positive in attitude, and filled with a spirit of cooperation. Jerry, you are a man filled with those attributes and you shared them very enthusiastically and effectively with our group."
- Letter from James F. Flynn, Vice President/General Manager/ Silicones, Union Carbide Corporation

"Your story is one that inspires us all to truly see what we are capable of doing, even when we feel that we are encumbered with obstacles too great to overcome. To set our goals before us and know that we can achieve them, that is what we are striving for."
- Letter from Terry Berrington, Development Leader, American Express - Travel Related Services

"Your insight into human nature and your motivational abilities are just too beautiful to describe in writing, but the looks on the faces of all who heard you that evening told the story loud and clear. We can't wait to have you back again. . ."
- Letter from Ellen Caruso, Colorado Chapter, American Physical Therapy Assn.

Jerry's corporate website is jerrytraylor.com. For an extensive list of corporate clients, visit www.jerrytraylor.com/clients.html.

Education Programs

A day with Jerry Traylor will open many eyes. Jerry's story is truly one that will capture the hearts of those who hear it. An imperfect man in a world demanding perfection; Jerry provides a real-life example of what success really means. His humor and heart leave an indelible impact on many as he journeys through the day... teaching others that their uniqueness is a gift rather than a curse.

Jerry will share his message with a variety of groups, while mainly focusing on public schools. He will challenge the thinking of those who are fortunate enough to hear his words. He will break down perceptions that are commonly held regarding health, happiness and success. The smaller group interaction following the assembly program is designed to pierce the armor of uncertainty and low self-esteem that has shadowed many. He tends to make every individual he comes in contact with see some possibilities and direction that they had been blinded to. All of us can change the world if we decide to discover and follow who we truly are rather than trying to be who others think we should be. Jerry's message and personal interaction open our hearts to self discovery and positive change.

Assembly Program:

This powerful message is centered on values necessary for personal growth. Jerry's pictorial essay detailing his successful run across America and climb up 14,110 foot Pikes Peak in Colorado will touch the heart of even the most jaded listener. What many would perceive to be a handicap has turned out to be a blessing.

Jerry listens to a middle-school student after an assembly.

His accomplishments, real-life example, powerful words and very real caring take away excuses; while opening up much needed self examination and dialogue. In the words of one educator... "Jerry provided a kick in the rear disguised as a hug!"

Some of the values that Jerry brings forth and exemplifies are: integrity, honesty, commitment, character, respect, compassion and cooperation. He focuses on the importance of making positive choices, choosing positive role models, having a good attitude and getting a good education.

The second stage of Jerry's strategy is classroom visitation and small group involvement. In this more intimate setting he examines thinking that leads to choices, both positive and negative. He prompts students thinking as he offers a new perspective and evidence drawn from his unique example. He teaches the power of positive choices and visions. He facilitates discussion (often in small groups) that is made much easier by his own transparency and caring. He challenges students to take ownership and helps each realize the relationship between positive choices and future opportunities. These smaller sessions should be limited to 100 or so individuals and seem to have the most impact on at-risk kids, although many student leaders have also been powerfully affected.

The following workshops are designed for smaller groups and are generally used in conjunction with Jerry's assembly or keynote program. They are effective whether working with the general population or student leaders. Jerry tailors each program with age appropriate material and individually for special needs and high risk students.

Becoming a Care-Actor (Character Education): A certain lifestyle and set of actions are necessary for the transformation from child to adulthood. Respect, Responsibility, Integrity, Cooperation and Compassion are values that contribute to our success. Many kids do not have this behavior modeled in their homes and therefore follow negative paths that halt the progress towards identifying their true potential. Schools have shown a marked improvement in student behavior, academic achievement and the attitude of staff with the implementation of character education programming.

Leading, Listening Leadership: Jerry believes that leaders do not simply run away from the pack... they get others excited about their vision; delegating and believing in others as they strive towards creating an environment that is conducive to learning and success. Jerry teaches skills that are necessary for successful leadership. Among these are listening, high expectations, and belief in oneself and the team. Whether it is your local student leadership, or state conferences such as Student Council, National Beta Club, Golden Key or National Honor Society, Jerry's words and example will help empower you and your team.

<u>G</u>o <u>O</u>ut <u>A</u>nd <u>L</u>ive <u>S</u>uccessfully (Goal-setting): Setting goals and having vision allows us to go the beyond the expectations of others and really create greatness in this world. In small group discussion, Jerry helps participants define their goals and take a closer look at them. Are they realistic? Is there a need for intermediate steps along the way? Have we identified and located the resources we will need for the journey? Jerry Traylor is an individual who leads by example.

<u>ME</u>aning and <u>YOU</u>niqueness (Diversity training): Jerry offers a pre-workshop survey designed to examine the attitudes we possess towards human differences and uses his unique prospective as a 'disabled' individual to teach lessons that effect positive change and cooperation.

Educational In-service Programs

"Enjoying the Fruit of our Labor"

This program comes straight from Jerry's heart. As a third grader, Jerry polished an apple for his teacher because she likewise saw the shine he possessed. Long before the implementation of Public Law 94.142 mandating integration into the least restrictive classroom setting, this caring teacher helped Jerry get to the core of his unique situation and helped plant the seeds of hope, self-confidence and coping skills. Because of her caring, the seeds have produced incredible fruit. This touching program provides an example of how you make a difference every day. This is a powerful keynote message for administrators, career education coordinators, special educators, Title One Facilitators and Adult Education Specialists.

Parent Program

"It's Ap-*parent* how important you are!"

Jerry Traylor credits his parents and other caring adults with shaping the attitude which he carries today. As educators we realize the impact that parents have when they team with their child's classroom teacher and staff.

During this workshop Jerry will take parents through "Ten Ways to Empower Your Children."

This program is a popular workshop at parenting conferences following Jerry's keynote address, and may be offered through community groups or the PTA for evening programs

For more information, visit jerrytraylor.com/education.html.

Help Spread the Message of Caring.

What actions and experiences have changed YOUR life? Please submit stories of caring that have taken place in your family life, at school, at work, or in your faith community. Jerry Traylor would love to publish your story of the impact these individuals and events have had on you and your loved ones. Submit your stories for consideration in future volumes:

Live *JOY*fully
Live *PLAY*fully
Live *HELP*fully
Live *FAITH*fully
Live *PRAYER*fully

U.S. Mail to:
13826 N. Cambria Unit B
Fountain Hills, AZ 85268

Or email to:
liveCAREfully@aol.com